T0078113

Precious HOLY SPIRIT

THE COMFORTER

HALCOURTH O'GILVIE

authorHOUSE®

AuthorHouse™
1663 Liberty Drive
Bloomington, IN 47403
www.authorhouse.com
Phone: 833-262-8899

Published by AuthorHouse 08/12/2020

ISBN: 978-1-7283-6845-0 (sc)
ISBN: 978-1-7283-6999-0 (e)

Print information available on the last page.

Any people depicted in stock imagery provided by Getty Images are models, and such images are being used for illustrative purposes only. Certain stock imagery © Getty Images.

This book is printed on acid-free paper.

NIV
Scripture quotations marked NIV are taken from the Holy Bible, New International Version®. NIV®. Copyright © 1973, 1978, 1984 by International Bible Society. Used by permission of Zondervan. All rights reserved. [Biblica]

NRSV
Scripture quotations marked NRSV are taken from the New Revised Standard Version of the Bible, Copyright © 1989, by the Division of Christian Education of the National Council of the Churches of Christ in the United States of America. Used by permission. All rights reserved. Website

CONTENTS

PRECIOUS HOLY SPIRIT

Obedience is the key to the Heart of Our Heavenly Father and His Precious Holy Spirit is there to lead us into all Truths.

1 Samuel 15:22 New International Version (NIV)
But Samuel replied: "Does the Lord delight in burnt offerings and sacrifice as much as in obeying the Lord? To obey is better than sacrifice, and to heed is better than the fat of rams."

John 16:13 NIV
But when he, the Spirit of truth, comes, he will guide you into all the truth. He will not speak on his own; he will speak only what he hears, and he will tell you what is yet to come.

ACKNOWLEDGEMENT

If we want to find abundant favour with Our Heavenly Father, we must surrender to His Precious Holy Spirit. Our Precious Saviour promised, "15 If you love me, keep my commands. 16 And I will ask the Father, and he will give you another advocate to help you and be with you forever." John 14:15-16 NIV

Without reservation, I have to give all credit to Our Precious Holy Spirit for helping me to write these words of encouragement. I have to confess, I was hesitant but He was persistent.

Special thanks go to my sister Chenieve O'Gilvie (aka my second mom). Chenieve, I am forever thankful to you for all that you do. I pray Our Heavenly Father's Blessings upon you for your obedience.

FOREWORDS

"But you will receive power when the Holy Spirit has come upon you; and you will be my witnesses in Jerusalem, in all Judea and Samaria, and to the ends of the earth." Acts 1:8 New Revised Standard Version (NRSV)

"But the Advocate, the Holy Spirit, whom the Father will send in my name, will teach you everything, and remind you of all that I have said to you." John 14:26 NRSV

It was about three years ago that I first met brother Halcourth O'Gilvie at one of our mutual friend's house which was the beginning of a great friendship. We soon found that we had many things in common. Halcourth not only loves the Lord Jesus Christ with all his heart but he is also passionate about helping others, especially the less privileged believers around the worldwide Church. It was his passion to help the poor and needy and an earnest desire to share the gospel with others that led him to join me on a mission trip to Karuna Ministries, India, in the fall of 2017. We both had an amazing time travelling, lodging, and ministering together in several cities and villages of northern India. It was during this trip that I came to know him closely as a person of deep faith. Almost daily, Halcourth would rise quite early in the morning and after spending time in the Scriptures he would begin composing his poems. Therefore, I know for sure that his writing comes out of his personal devotions and his meditations on the Word of God. There is nothing philosophical or theoretical about his poems, but a humble reflection on the Word that relates to his personal walk with the Lord.

I am; therefore, very happy to have gone through the initial manuscript of Halcourth's second book, Precious Holy Spirit, which continues the same form and passion demonstrated in his first book, Precious Jesus. It shows a deeper grasp of the Holy Spirit and His working in a believer's life. It is a humble prayer to the Holy Spirit. It is a plea to the Holy Spirit for forgiveness, seeking more of His power and strength to live for Him and for His glory. I believe with all my heart that Precious Holy Spirit would help the reader hear the heartbeat of the Holy Spirit and make you want more of Him in your life as it has done to Halcourth. Therefore, I heartily recommend this book to all who want to walk in step with the Holy Spirit. If, like me, you ever run out of words and phrases to pray, or just do not know how to pray, this book will greatly help you in your prayer life and will bring you closer to God the Almighty.

Rev. Dr. Vinod John
Founding Director
Karuna Ministries, India

God has given me a brother, a friend, a man with such passion and effectiveness for the advancement of the Kingdom of God through the spreading of the gospel of Jesus Christ. It was a very delightful moment when I first met brother Halcourth O'Gilvie, the summer of 2016 in Kingston, Jamaica, through a mutual friend. Our friendship developed over the years, and I soon discovered his passion for souls, the needy and the marginalized, that made such a difference with those he comes in contact with.

He is driven with compassion to make a difference where ever he goes. God has graced him in the area of evangelism and through his writings of poems and books, many lives has been transformed and encouraged.

I received a copy of his first book when we first met, Precious Jesus, that still resonates with me today. After reading through the initial manuscript of his second book, Precious Holy Spirit, I'm excited and believe it will be a tremendous blessing to its readers.

Therefore, I highly recommend this book to anyone that desires to have a closer and more intimate walk with the Holy Spirit.

Rev. Dr. Fred Mitchell
Founder Arkcompassionate Ministry
President U.O.M.I Ministry
International Overseas Of LCGCC
International Director for Development of Regency School of Ministry and Mission

PRECIOUS HOLY SPIRIT

PRECIOUS HOLY SPIRIT, PLEASE RESCUE ME. PLEASE TEACH ME OF THINGS MY EYES CANNOT SEE.

PRECIOUS HOLY SPIRIT, PLEASE BLESS ME. PLEASE BLESS ME SO THE WORLD CAN SEE MORE OF YOU AND LESS OF ME.

PRECIOUS HOLY SPIRIT, PLEASE NURTURE ME. PLEASE NURTURE ME SO YOU CAN SET ME FREE.

PRECIOUS HOLY SPIRIT, PLEASE WASH ME. PLEASE WASH ME SO I CAN BE CLEANSED SOLELY FOR THEE.

PRECIOUS HOLY SPIRIT, PLEASE LIFT ME UP. PLEASE LIFT ME UP AND WITH THEE I WILL SUPP.

PRECIOUS HOLY SPIRIT, PLEASE DIRECT MY WAY. PLEASE DIRECT MY WAY AND NEVER LET ME FRAY.

PRECIOUS HOLY SPIRIT, PLEASE CALL MY NAME. PLEASE CALL MY NAME AND IN YOU, I WILL FOREVER REMAIN.

PRECIOUS HOLY SPIRIT, PLEASE HELP ME TO KNOW YOU BETTER, EVERY SECOND OF EVERY HOUR OF EVERY DAY. I ASK THIS IN THE MIGHTY NAME OF JESUS. AMEN AND AMEN.

PRECIOUS HOLY SPIRIT, PLEASE TAKE AWAY MY FEARS

PRECIOUS HOLY SPIRIT, PLEASE TAKE AWAY MY FEARS, PLEASE TAKE AWAY MY DOUBTS. PLEASE TAKE AWAY THE DESTRUCTIONS THAT THE DEVIL IS ALL ABOUT.

PRECIOUS HOLY SPIRIT, PLEASE TAKE AWAY MY PAIN, PLEASE TAKE AWAY MY STRAIN. PLEASE TAKE AWAY ANYTHING THAT WOULD MAKE ME INSANE.

PRECIOUS HOLY SPIRIT, PLEASE TAKE AWAY WHAT MAKES ME BLIND, PLEASE TAKE AWAY WHAT MAKES ME UNKIND. PLEASE TAKE AWAY ALL THAT IS NOT OF YOUR MIND.

PRECIOUS HOLY SPIRIT, PLEASE TAKE AWAY MY RAGE, PLEASE TAKE AWAY MY GAGE. PLEASE TAKE AWAY ALL THAT WOULD KEEP ME FROM YOUR STAGE.

PRECIOUS HOLY SPIRIT, PLEASE TAKE AWAY STAIN, PLEASE TAKE AWAY SHAME. PLEASE REPLACE IT ALL WITH JESUS PRECIOUS HOLY NAME.

PRECIOUS HOLY SPIRIT, PLEASE TAKE AWAY MY ANGER, PLEASE TAKE AWAY MY SLANDER. PLEASE TAKE AWAY ALL THAT IS NOT OF MY KING AND COMMANDER.

PRECIOUS HOLY SPIRIT, PLEASE TAKE AWAY MY FROWN, PLEASE TAKE AWAY ALL THAT KEEPS ME DOWN. PLEASE REPLACE IT WITH MY FATHER'S EVERLASTING CROWN.

PRECIOUS HOLY SPIRIT, PLEASE TAKE AWAY ALL THAT IS NOT RIGHT, PLEASE TAKE AWAY ALL THAT IS NOT BRIGHT. PLEASE LEAD ME TO JESUS FOR THE REST OF MY DAYS SO I CAN GIVE HIM ALL OF MY PRAISE. I ASK THIS PRECIOUS HOLY SPIRIT IN THE PRECIOUS NAME OF JESUS. AMEN AND AMEN.

PLEASE FILL MY HEART PRECIOUS HOLY SPIRIT

PLEASE FILL MY HEART PRECIOUS HOLY SPIRIT AND MAY YOU NEVER DEPART PRECIOUS HOLY SPIRIT, I PRAY.

PLEASE FILL MY MIND PRECIOUS HOLY SPIRIT AND MAKE IT LIKE UNTO THINE PRECIOUS HOLY SPIRIT, I PRAY.

PLEASE FILL MY HANDS PRECIOUS HOLY SPIRIT AND MAKE ME WALK ACCORDING TO YOUR ETERNAL PLANS PRECIOUS HOLY SPIRIT, I PRAY.

PLEASE FILL MY SIGHT PRECIOUS HOLY SPIRIT AND HELP ME TO ACCOMPLISH ALL ACCORDING TO YOUR MIGHT PRECIOUS HOLY SPIRIT, I PRAY.

PLEASE FILL MY DAY PRECIOUS HOLY SPIRIT AND GUIDE ME ALONG THE WAY PRECIOUS HOLY SPIRIT, I PRAY.

PLEASE FILL MY HOUR PRECIOUS HOLY SPIRIT AND UPHOLD ME WITH YOUR ETERNAL POWER PRECIOUS HOLY SPIRIT, I PRAY.

PLEASE FILL MY MOMENT PRECIOUS HOLY SPIRIT AND CHRIST SHALL BE MY EVERLASTING ATONEMENT PRECIOUS HOLY SPIRIT, I PRAY.

PRECIOUS HOLY SPIRIT, PLEASE FILL ME WITH YOUR EVERLASTING LOVE AND POWER. PLEASE HELP ME TO DEPEND ON YOU EACH AND EVERY HOUR, I PRAY IN JESUS MIGHTY NAME. AMEN AND AMEN.

PLEASE HELP ME PRECIOUS HOLY SPIRIT

PLEASE HELP ME PRECIOUS HOLY SPIRIT TO SEE WITH YOUR EYES WHAT MY EYES CANNOT SEE.

PLEASE HELP ME PRECIOUS HOLY SPIRIT TO DO WITH YOUR HANDS WHAT MY HANDS CANNOT DO.

PLEASE HELP ME PRECIOUS HOLY SPIRIT TO HEAR WITH YOUR EARS WHAT MY EARS CANNOT HEAR.

PLEASE HELP ME PRECIOUS HOLY SPIRIT TO SPEAK WITH YOUR MOUTH WHAT MY MOUTH CANNOT SPEAK.

PLEASE HELP ME PRECIOUS HOLY SPIRIT TO LOVE WITH YOUR LOVE WHAT I CANNOT LOVE.

PLEASE HELP ME PRECIOUS HOLY SPIRIT TO GIVE OF YOUR PEACE WHICH I CANNOT GIVE.

PLEASE HELP ME PRECIOUS HOLY SPIRIT TO LIVE LIKE YOU LIVE THE LIFE I CANNOT LIVE.

PRECIOUS HOLY SPIRIT, I AM DESPERATE FOR YOUR HELP. SPIRIT OF THE LIVING GOD, I NEED TO DO AS YOU DO AND FOLLOW ONLY AFTER YOU. I ASK THIS IN THE MIGHTY NAME OF JESUS. AMEN AND AMEN.

PRECIOUS HOLY SPIRIT PLEASE LEAD ME

PRECIOUS HOLY SPIRIT, PLEASE LEAD ME OUT OF THIS RUT. I NEED YOU TO GIVE ME A SWIFT KICK IN THE BUTT.

PRECIOUS HOLY SPIRIT, PLEASE LEAD ME OUT OF THIS DOWNWARD SPIRAL. I NEED YOU TO BE MY GUIDING ADMIRAL.

PRECIOUS HOLY SPIRIT, PLEASE LEAD ME OUT OF THIS PLACE. I NEED YOU TO ELIMINATE THE TIMES THAT I WASTE.

PRECIOUS HOLY SPIRIT, PLEASE LEAD ME TO THE TOP. I NEED YOU TO BREAK MY FALL WHEN I DROP.

PRECIOUS HOLY SPIRIT, PLEASE LEAD ME TO LOVE YOU. I NEED TO KEEP FROM PLACING ANYONE ABOVE YOU.

PRECIOUS HOLY SPIRIT, PLEASE LEAD ME TO YOUR REST. I NEED YOUR GUIDANCE TO PASS LIFE'S TEST.

PRECIOUS HOLY SPIRIT, PLEASE LEAD ME TO YOUR ARMS. I NEED TO FEEL YOUR LOVING CHARMS.

PRECIOUS HOLY SPIRIT IN ALL THAT I DO, I WILL ACKNOWLEDGE YOU. THANK YOU FOR BEING MY GUIDING LIGHT AND MY SOURCE OF STRENGTH. I WILL GIVE YOU ALL OF MY PRAISE FOR THE REST OF MY DAYS. I SAY THIS IN THE MOST PRECIOUS NAME OF JESUS. AMEN AND AMEN.

MY SPIRIT HUNGERS FOR YOU PRECIOUS HOLY SPIRIT

MY SPIRIT HUNGERS FOR YOU PRECIOUS HOLY SPIRIT MORE THAN WORDS COULD SAY. MY SPIRIT HUNGERS FOR YOU PRECIOUS HOLY SPIRIT PLEASE SATISFY MY YEARNING TODAY.

MY SPIRIT HUNGERS FOR YOU PRECIOUS HOLY SPIRIT I AM DESPERATE TO HEAR YOUR VOICE. MY SPIRIT HUNGERS FOR YOU PRECIOUS HOLY SPIRIT, I AM LONGING TO MAKE YOU MY CHOICE.

MY SPIRIT HUNGERS FOR YOU PRECIOUS HOLY SPIRIT AS I AWAKE IN THE EARLY MORNING. MY SPIRIT HUNGERS FOR YOU PRECIOUS HOLY SPIRIT, I LONG FOR YOUR GLORIOUS ADORNING.

MY SPIRIT HUNGERS FOR YOU PRECIOUS HOLY SPIRIT I HUNGER FOR YOU AT NOON. MY SPIRIT HUNGERS FOR YOU PRECIOUS HOLY SPIRIT PLEASE SATISFY THIS HUNGER SOON.

MY SPIRIT HUNGERS FOR YOU PRECIOUS HOLY SPIRIT I HUNGER FOR YOU AT NIGHT. MY SPIRIT HUNGERS FOR YOU PRECIOUS HOLY SPIRIT PLEASE SATISFY ME WITH YOUR ETERNAL MIGHT.

MY SPIRIT HUNGERS FOR YOU PRECIOUS HOLY SPIRIT EACH AND EVERY WAKING HOUR. MY SPIRIT HUNGERS FOR YOU PRECIOUS HOLY SPIRIT, PLEASE BLESS ME WITH YOUR EVERLASTING POWER.

MY SPIRIT HUNGERS FOR YOU PRECIOUS HOLY SPIRIT I NEED YOU TO FILL MY SOUL. MY SPIRIT HUNGERS FOR YOU PRECIOUS HOLY SPIRIT PLEASE FILL ME AND MAKE ME BOLD.

PRECIOUS JESUS, I AM HUNGRY FOR YOU. PLEASE HELP ME AND GUIDE ME TO THE THINGS THAT ARE PLEASING ONLY TO YOU. I ASK THIS IN YOUR PRECIOUS HOLY NAME JESUS. AMEN AND AMEN.

PRECIOUS HOLY SPIRIT, PLEASE FORGIVE ME FOR INSULTING YOU

PRECIOUS HOLY SPIRIT, PLEASE FORGIVE ME FOR INSULTING YOU AND FOR MY LIMITED THOUGHTS, I HAVE OF YOU.

PRECIOUS HOLY SPIRIT, PLEASE FORGIVE ME FOR INSULTING YOU AND FOR THE DOUBT THAT IS WITHIN MY HEART TOWARDS YOU.

PRECIOUS HOLY SPIRIT, PLEASE FORGIVE ME FOR INSULTING YOU AND FOR DEPENDING ON MANKIND INSTEAD OF YOU.

PRECIOUS HOLY SPIRIT, PLEASE FORGIVE ME FOR INSULTING YOU AND FOR MY DESPERATION INSTEAD OF ASKING OF YOU.

PRECIOUS HOLY SPIRIT, PLEASE FORGIVE ME FOR INSULTING YOU AND FOR NOT COUNTING MY BLESSINGS THAT CAME FROM YOU.

PRECIOUS HOLY SPIRIT, PLEASE FORGIVE ME FOR INSULTING YOU AND FOR MY SHORTSIGHTEDNESS I HAVE TOWARDS YOU.

PRECIOUS HOLY SPIRIT, PLEASE FORGIVE ME FOR INSULTING YOU BECAUSE THERE IS NO BETTER COMFORTER I HAVE BESIDES YOU.

I THANK YOU PRECIOUS HOLY SPIRIT THAT YOU WILL NEVER DISAPPOINT ME. I THANK YOU THAT LIFE LESSONS HAVE THOUGHT ME TO BE COMFORTED BY YOU. I THANK YOU FOR BLESSING ME PRECIOUS HEAVENLY FATHER. I THANK YOU FOR BLESSING ME PRECIOUS JESUS. I PRAY THIS IN THE PRECIOUS MIGHTY NAME OF JESUS. AMEN AND AMEN.

PLEASE TURN MY WATER INTO WINE PRECIOUS HOLY SPIRIT

PLEASE TURN MY WATER INTO WINE PRECIOUS HOLY SPIRIT,
PLEASE TEACH ME THY WAYS FOR THE REST OF MY DAYS.

PLEASE TURN MY WATER INTO WINE PRECIOUS HOLY SPIRIT,
PLEASE TEACH ME TO LOVE AS YOU WATCH ME FROM ABOVE.

PLEASE TURN MY WATER INTO WINE PRECIOUS HOLY SPIRIT,
PLEASE TEACH ME TO SHARE AND SHOW ME HOW MUCH YOU
CARE.

PLEASE TURN MY WATER INTO WINE PRECIOUS HOLY SPIRIT,
PLEASE TEACH ME TO PRAY AS I GO FROM DAY TO DAY.

PLEASE TURN MY WATER INTO WINE PRECIOUS HOLY SPIRIT,
PLEASE TEACH ME TO ASK BEFORE I TAKE UP MY DAILY TASK.

PLEASE TURN MY WATER INTO WINE PRECIOUS HOLY SPIRIT,
PLEASE TEACH ME TO HOPE AS YOU BROADEN MY SCOPE.

PLEASE TURN MY WATER INTO WINE PRECIOUS HOLY SPIRIT,
PLEASE TEACH ME TO PRAY AND NEVER TO GO ASTRAY.

I THANK YOU PRECIOUS HOLY SPIRIT FOR COMING INTO MY
LIFE AND FOR TURNING MY WATER INTO WINE. PLEASE HELP
ME TO BE FAITHFUL TO MY HEAVENLY FATHER AND MY LORD
AND SAVIOUR JESUS. I PRAY THIS IN THE MIGHTY NAME OF
JESUS. AMEN AND AMEN.

FALL ON ME PRECIOUS HOLY SPIRIT

FALL ON ME PRECIOUS HOLY SPIRIT, I NEED YOUR POWER
EACH AND EVERY HOUR.

FALL ON ME PRECIOUS HOLY SPIRIT, I NEED YOU NEAR TO
HELP TAKE AWAY MY FEAR.

FALL ON ME PRECIOUS HOLY SPIRIT, I NEED YOU CLOSE SO I
CAN LOVE YOU THE MOST.

FALL ON ME PRECIOUS HOLY SPIRIT, I NEED YOUR LOVE AND
YOUR BLESSINGS FROM ABOVE.

FALL ON ME PRECIOUS HOLY SPIRIT, I NEED YOUR GRACE AND
THE GLORY THAT SURROUNDS YOUR FACE.

FALL ON ME PRECIOUS HOLY SPIRIT, I NEED YOUR HEART AND
FORBID ME NEVER TO DEPART.

FALL ON ME PRECIOUS HOLY SPIRIT, I NEED YOUR PERFECTION
IN MY EVERY DIRECTION.

PRECIOUS HOLY SPIRIT, PLEASE FALL ON ME AND COMFORT
ME. PLEASE HELP ME PRECIOUS HOLY SPIRIT TO DEPEND ON
YOU JUST LIKE MY SAVIOUR DID. I LONG FOR YOUR WARM
EMBRACE AND YOUR AMAZING GRACE. I PRAY THIS IN THE
MIGHTY NAME OF JESUS. AMEN AND AMEN.

HEAL ME PRECIOUS HOLY SPIRIT

HEAL ME PRECIOUS HOLY SPIRIT WHILE I AM YIELDED AND STILL.

HEAL ME PRECIOUS HOLY SPIRIT AND HELP ME TO ACCOMPLISH YOUR WILL.

HEAL ME PRECIOUS HOLY SPIRIT SO I CAN DO WHAT IS GOOD.

HEAL ME PRECIOUS HOLY SPIRIT SO I CAN LOVE YOU LIKE I SHOULD.

HEAL ME PRECIOUS HOLY SPIRIT SO I CAN DO WHAT IS RIGHT.

HEAL ME PRECIOUS HOLY SPIRIT SO I CAN BE BLESSED BY YOUR MIGHT.

HEAL ME PRECIOUS HOLY SPIRIT SO I CAN SHOW YOUR LOVE.

HEAL ME PRECIOUS HOLY SPIRIT SO YOU CAN RESCUE ME FROM ABOVE.

HEAL ME PRECIOUS HOLY SPIRIT SO I CAN BE MADE NEW.

HEAL ME PRECIOUS HOLY SPIRIT SO I CAN CLING ONLY TO YOU.

HEAL ME PRECIOUS HOLY SPIRIT SO I CAN SEE YOUR FACE.

HEAL ME PRECIOUS HOLY SPIRIT SO I CAN TASTE OF YOUR GRACE.

HEAL ME PRECIOUS HOLY SPIRIT WHILE I AM WAITING HERE.

HEAL ME PRECIOUS HOLY SPIRIT AND DRAW ME EVER SO NEAR.

I THANK YOU PRECIOUS HOLY SPIRIT FOR HEALING ME. SPIRIT OF THE LIVING GOD, I ADORE YOU AND I HONOUR YOU FOR ALL THAT YOU DO. I PRAY THIS IN THE MIGHTY NAME OF JESUS. AMEN AND AMEN.

BREATHE UPON ME PRECIOUS HOLY SPIRIT

SPIRIT OF LOVE PLEASE BREATHE UPON ME THY POWER FROM ABOVE.

SPIRIT OF MIGHT PLEASE BREATHE UPON ME EVERYTHING THAT IS RIGHT.

SPIRIT OF HOPE PLEASE BREATHE UPON ME YOUR ETERNAL SCOPE.

SPIRIT OF POWER PLEASE BREATHE UPON ME EACH AND EVERY HOUR.

SPIRIT OF LIGHT PLEASE BREATHE UPON ME EVERYTHING THAT IS BRIGHT.

SPIRIT OF HEALTH PLEASE BREATHE UPON ME YOUR ETERNAL WEALTH.

SPIRIT OF BLESSINGS PLEASE BREATHE UPON ME AND TEACH ME YOUR ETERNAL LESSONS.

SPIRIT OF THE LIVING GOD, I KNOW MY HOPE IS IN YOU.
SPIRIT OF THE LIVING GOD, I KNOW MY JOY IS IN YOU.
SPIRIT OF THE LIVING GOD, I KNOW MY ALL IS IN YOU.
SPIRIT OF THE LIVING GOD, I AM CALLING OUT TO YOU, PLEASE ANSWER. I APPRECIATE YOU IN THE NAME OF THE FATHER AND THE SON. AMEN AND AMEN.

PRECIOUS HOLY SPIRIT, I NEED SOMETHING THAT LASTS

PRECIOUS HOLY SPIRIT, I NEED SOMETHING THAT LASTS. I NEED THE LOVE OF THE FATHER, TODAY AND FOREVER AFTER.

PRECIOUS HOLY SPIRIT, I NEED SOMETHING THAT LASTS. I NEED THE FATHER'S BLESSINGS FROM ABOVE TO REST UPON ME LIKE A GENTLE DOVE.

PRECIOUS HOLY SPIRIT, I NEED SOMETHING THAT LASTS. I NEED THE FATHER'S GRACE ALONG WITH HIS SMILING FACE.

PRECIOUS HOLY SPIRIT, I NEED SOMETHING THAT LASTS. I NEED THE FATHER'S POWER, EVERY DAY, EVERY MINUTE AND EVERY HOUR.

PRECIOUS HOLY SPIRIT, I NEED SOMETHING THAT LASTS. I NEED THE FATHER'S TOUCH I LONG FOR IT EVER SO MUCH.

PRECIOUS HOLY SPIRIT, I NEED SOMETHING THAT LASTS. I NEED THE FATHER'S HAND TO GUIDE ME TOWARDS HIS ETERNAL PLAN.

PRECIOUS HOLY SPIRIT, I NEED SOMETHING THAT LASTS. I NEED THE FATHER'S GLORY SO I CAN TELL HIS SALVATION'S STORY.

PRECIOUS HOLY SPIRIT, I NEED SOMETHING THAT LASTS. PRECIOUS HOLY SPIRIT I NEED YOU. MY JESUS SAID, YOU WILL BE MY COMFORTER, YOU WILL TEACH ME WHAT TO SAY AND YOU WILL GUIDE ME INTO ALL TRUTHS. I CLAIM THESE PROMISES IN THE MIGHTY NAME OF JESUS. AMEN AND AMEN.

PLEASE HEAL MY HEART PRECIOUS HOLY SPIRIT

THE FRIENDS I ONCE HAD, HAS MADE MY HEART SO SAD. PLEASE HEAL MY HEART PRECIOUS HOLY SPIRIT.

THE LAUGHTER I ONCE ENJOYED, THE ENEMY HAS DESTROYED. PLEASE HEAL MY HEART PRECIOUS HOLY SPIRIT.

THE FELLOWSHIP I ONCE CHERISHED HAS SLIPPED AWAY AND PERISHED. PLEASE HEAL MY HEART PRECIOUS HOLY SPIRIT.

THE ADVISORS I ONCE KNEW HAS MADE MY DAYS SO BLUE. PLEASE HEAL MY HEART PRECIOUS HOLY SPIRIT.

THE PAIN I HAVE SUSTAINED I CANNOT AFFORT TO RETAIN. PLEASE HEAL MY HEART PRECIOUS HOLY SPIRIT.

THE HURT I NOW FEEL TO THE SPIRIT I WILL APPEAL. PLEASE HEAL MY HEART PRECIOUS HOLY SPIRIT.

THE COMFORTER IS HERE WITH ME, THE SON HAS SET ME FREE. THANK YOU FOR HEALING MY HEART PRECIOUS HOLY SPIRIT.

PRECIOUS JESUS, I THANK YOU FOR SENDING ME YOUR PRECIOUS HOLY SPIRIT. YOU PRECIOUS HOLY SPIRIT HAVE BEEN MY COMFORT AND MY JOY. I THANK YOU FOR YOUR LOVE PRECIOUS HOLY FATHER, I THANK YOU FOR YOUR SACRIFICE PRECIOUS LORD JESUS, I THANK YOU FOR YOUR COMFORT PRECIOUS HOLY SPIRIT. IN THE MIGHTY NAME OF JESUS, I PRAY THIS. AMEN AND AMEN.

I THANK YOU PRECIOUS HOLY SPIRIT FOR PROSPERING ME

I THANK YOU PRECIOUS HOLY SPIRIT FOR PROSPERING ME. I THANK YOU FOR OPENING MY EYES SO I CAN SEE.

I THANK YOU PRECIOUS HOLY SPIRIT FOR PROSPERING ME. I THANK YOU FOR SHOWING ME THE FATHER'S LOVE THAT HAS SET ME FREE.

I THANK YOU PRECIOUS HOLY SPIRIT FOR PROSPERING ME. I THANK YOU FOR SHOWING ME JESUS WHO BLED AND DIED FOR ME.

I THANK YOU PRECIOUS HOLY SPIRIT FOR PROSPERING ME. I THANK YOU FOR YOUR LOVING KINDNESS AND YOUR TENDER MERCIES SO THAT ALL EYES CAN SEE.

I THANK YOU PRECIOUS HOLY SPIRIT FOR PROSPERING ME. I THANK YOU FOR YOUR GLORY THAT HAS LIBERATED ME.

I THANK YOU PRECIOUS HOLY SPIRIT FOR PROSPERING ME. I THANK YOU FOR YOUR GUIDANCE AND PROTECTION THAT RESIDES OVER ME.

I THANK YOU PRECIOUS HOLY SPIRIT FOR PROSPERING ME. I THANK YOU FOR WHAT MY FATHER HAS IN STORE FOR ME.

SPIRIT OF THE LIVING GOD, I APPRECIATE YOU. SPIRIT OF THE LIVING GOD, I ADORE YOU. SPIRIT OF THE LIVIG GOD, I LOVE YOU. THANK YOU PRECIOUS HOLY SPIRIT FOR SHOWING ME LOVE AND THE THINGS OF MY HEAVENLY FATHER UP ABOVE. I APPRECIATE THIS IN THE MIGHTY NAME OF JESUS. AMEN AND AMEN.

PLEASE TEACH ME HOW TO OPEN THE DOOR OF HOPE PRECIOUS HOLY SPIRIT

PLEASE TEACH ME HOW TO OPEN THE DOOR OF HOPE PRECIOUS HOLY SPIRIT. PLEASE TEACH ME WHAT TO DO, AND HOW TO DEPEND ONLY ON YOU.

PLEASE TEACH ME HOW TO OPEN THE DOOR OF HOPE PRECIOUS HOLY SPIRIT. PLEASE TEACH ME HOW TO SOAR AND REMIND ME OF THE THINGS THAT YOU ADORE.

PLEASE TEACH ME HOW TO OPEN THE DOOR OF HOPE PRECIOUS HOLY SPIRIT. PLEASE TEACH ME HOW TO LOVE AND TO FOCUS ON THE THINGS FROM HEAVEN ABOVE.

PLEASE TEACH ME HOW TO OPEN THE DOOR OF HOPE PRECIOUS HOLY SPIRIT. PLEASE TEACH ME HOW TO SHARE BECAUSE I KNOW HOW MUCH YOU CARE.

PLEASE TEACH ME HOW TO OPEN THE DOOR OF HOPE PRECIOUS HOLY SPIRIT. PLEASE TEACH ME HOW TO BE STILL AS I DO THY ETERNAL WILL.

PLEASE TEACH ME HOW TO OPEN THE DOOR OF HOPE PRECIOUS HOLY SPIRIT. PLEASE TEACH ME HOW TO PRAISE AS I TURN MY EYES UPON YOU AND GAZE.

PLEASE TEACH ME HOW TO OPEN THE DOOR OF HOPE PRECIOUS HOLY SPIRIT. PLEASE TEACH ME HOW TO PRAY AS I GO FROM DAY TO DAY.

I THANK YOU PRECIOUS HOLY SPIRIT FOR OPENING THE DOOR OF HOPE FOR ME. IN YOU PRECIOUS HOLY SPIRIT, I CAN HOPE ALL THINGS THAT GLORIFY MY HEAVENLY FATHER. I GIVE YOU THANKS PRECIOUS HOLY SPIRIT IN THE MIGHTY NAME OF JESUS. AMEN AND AMEN.

PLEASE TEACH ME HOW TO OPEN THE DOOR OF FAITH PRECIOUS HOLY SPIRIT

PLEASE TEACH ME HOW TO OPEN THE DOOR OF FAITH PRECIOUS HOLY SPIRIT. PLEASE TEACH ME WHAT TO DO AND HOW TO DEPEND ONLY ON YOU.

PLEASE TEACH ME HOW TO OPEN THE DOOR OF FAITH PRECIOUS HOLY SPIRIT. PLEASE TEACH ME HOW TO SOAR AND REMIND ME OF THE THINGS THAT YOU ADORE.

PLEASE TEACH ME HOW TO OPEN THE DOOR OF FAITH PRECIOUS HOLY SPIRIT. PLEASE TEACH ME HOW TO LOVE AND TO FOCUS ON THE THINGS FROM HEAVEN ABOVE.

PLEASE TEACH ME HOW TO OPEN THE DOOR OF FAITH PRECIOUS HOLY SPIRIT. PLEASE TEACH ME HOW TO SHARE BECAUSE I KNOW HOW MUCH YOU CARE.

PLEASE TEACH ME HOW TO OPEN THE DOOR OF FAITH PRECIOUS HOLY SPIRIT. PLEASE TEACH ME HOW TO BE STILL AS I DO THY ETERNAL WILL.

PLEASE TEACH ME HOW TO OPEN THE DOOR OF FAITH PRECIOUS HOLY SPIRIT. PLEASE TEACH ME HOW TO PRAISE AS I TURN MY EYES UPON YOU AND GAZE.

PLEASE TEACH ME HOW TO OPEN THE DOOR OF FAITH PRECIOUS HOLY SPIRIT. PLEASE TEACH ME HOW TO PRAY AS I GO FROM DAY TO DAY.

I THANK YOU PRECIOUS HOLY SPIRIT FOR OPENING THE DOOR OF FAITH FOR ME. IN YOU PRECIOUS HOLY SPIRIT, I HAVE FAITH IN ALL THINGS THAT GLORIFY MY HEAVENLY FATHER. I GIVE YOU THANKS PRECIOUS HOLY SPIRIT IN THE MIGHTY NAME OF JESUS. AMEN AND AMEN.

PLEASE TEACH ME HOW TO OPEN THE DOOR OF LOVE PRECIOUS HOLY SPIRIT

PLEASE TEACH ME HOW TO OPEN THE DOOR OF LOVE PRECIOUS HOLY SPIRIT. PLEASE TEACH ME WHAT TO DO AND HOW TO DEPEND ONLY ON YOU.

PLEASE TEACH ME HOW TO OPEN THE DOOR OF LOVE PRECIOUS HOLY SPIRIT. PLEASE TEACH ME HOW TO SOAR AND REMIND ME OF THE THINGS THAT YOU ADORE.

PLEASE TEACH ME HOW TO OPEN THE DOOR OF LOVE PRECIOUS HOLY SPIRIT. PLEASE TEACH ME HOW TO LOVE AND TO FOCUS ON THE THINGS FROM HEAVEN ABOVE.

PLEASE TEACH ME HOW TO OPEN THE DOOR OF LOVE PRECIOUS HOLY SPIRIT. PLEASE TEACH ME HOW TO SHARE BECAUSE I KNOW HOW MUCH YOU CARE.

PLEASE TEACH ME HOW TO OPEN THE DOOR OF LOVE PRECIOUS HOLY SPIRIT. PLEASE TEACH ME HOW TO BE STILL AS I DO THY ETERNAL WILL.

PLEASE TEACH ME HOW TO OPEN THE DOOR OF LOVE PRECIOUS HOLY SPIRIT. PLEASE TEACH ME HOW TO PRAISE AS I TURN MY EYES UPON YOU AND GAZE.

PLEASE TEACH ME HOW TO OPEN THE DOOR OF LOVE PRECIOUS HOLY SPIRIT. PLEASE TEACH ME HOW TO PRAY AS I GO FROM DAY TO DAY.

I THANK YOU PRECIOUS HOLY SPIRIT FOR OPENING THE DOOR OF LOVE FOR ME. IN YOU PRECIOUS HOLY SPIRIT, I CAN LOVE ALL THINGS THAT GLORIFY MY HEAVENLY FATHER. I GIVE YOU THANKS PRECIOUS HOLY SPIRIT IN THE MIGHTY NAME OF JESUS. AMEN AND AMEN.

PLEASE TEACH ME HOW TO OPEN THE DOOR OF GRACE PRECIOUS HOLY SPIRIT

PLEASE TEACH ME HOW TO OPEN THE DOOR OF GRACE PRECIOUS HOLY SPIRIT. PLEASE TEACH ME WHAT TO DO AND HOW TO DEPEND ONLY ON YOU.

PLEASE TEACH ME HOW TO OPEN THE DOOR OF GRACE PRECIOUS HOLY SPIRIT. PLEASE TEACH ME HOW TO SOAR AND REMIND ME OF THE THINGS THAT YOU ADORE.

PLEASE TEACH ME HOW TO OPEN THE DOOR OF GRACE PRECIOUS HOLY SPIRIT. PLEASE TEACH ME HOW TO LOVE AND TO FOCUS ON THE THINGS FROM HEAVEN ABOVE.

PLEASE TEACH ME HOW TO OPEN THE DOOR OF GRACE PRECIOUS HOLY SPIRIT. PLEASE TEACH ME HOW TO SHARE BECAUSE I KNOW HOW MUCH YOU CARE.

PLEASE TEACH ME HOW TO OPEN THE DOOR OF GRACE PRECIOUS HOLY SPIRIT. PLEASE TEACH ME HOW TO BE STILL AS I DO THY ETERNAL WILL.

PLEASE TEACH ME HOW TO OPEN THE DOOR OF GRACE PRECIOUS HOLY SPIRIT. PLEASE TEACH ME HOW TO PRAISE AS I TURN MY EYES UPON YOU AND GAZE.

PLEASE TEACH ME HOW TO OPEN THE DOOR OF GRACE PRECIOUS HOLY SPIRIT. PLEASE TEACH ME HOW TO PRAY AS I GO FROM DAY TO DAY.

I THANK YOU PRECIOUS HOLY SPIRIT FOR OPENING THE DOOR OF GRACE FOR ME. IN YOU PRECIOUS HOLY SPIRIT, I AM GRATEFUL IN ALL THINGS THAT GLORIFY MY HEAVENLY FATHER. I GIVE YOU THANKS PRECIOUS HOLY SPIRIT IN THE MIGHTY NAME OF JESUS. AMEN AND AMEN.

PLEASE TEACH ME HOW TO OPEN THE DOOR OF MERCY PRECIOUS HOLY SPIRIT

PLEASE TEACH ME HOW TO OPEN THE DOOR OF MERCY PRECIOUS HOLY SPIRIT. PLEASE TEACH ME WHAT TO DO AND HOW TO DEPEND ONLY ON YOU.

PLEASE TEACH ME HOW TO OPEN THE DOOR OF MERCY PRECIOUS HOLY SPIRIT. PLEASE TEACH ME HOW TO SOAR AND REMIND ME OF THE THINGS THAT YOU ADORE.

PLEASE TEACH ME HOW TO OPEN THE DOOR OF MERCY PRECIOUS HOLY SPIRIT. PLEASE TEACH ME HOW TO LOVE AND TO FOCUS ON THE THINGS FROM HEAVEN ABOVE.

PLEASE TEACH ME HOW TO OPEN THE DOOR OF MERCY PRECIOUS HOLY SPIRIT. PLEASE TEACH ME HOW TO SHARE BECAUSE I KNOW HOW MUCH YOU CARE.

PLEASE TEACH ME HOW TO OPEN THE DOOR OF MERCY PRECIOUS HOLY SPIRIT. PLEASE TEACH ME HOW TO BE STILL AS I DO THY ETERNAL WILL.

PLEASE TEACH ME HOW TO OPEN THE DOOR OF MERCY PRECIOUS HOLY SPIRIT. PLEASE TEACH ME HOW TO PRAISE AS I TURN MY EYES UPON YOU AND GAZE.

PLEASE TEACH ME HOW TO OPEN THE DOOR OF MERCY PRECIOUS HOLY SPIRIT. PLEASE TEACH ME HOW TO PRAY AS I GO FROM DAY TO DAY.

I THANK YOU PRECIOUS HOLY SPIRIT FOR OPENING THE DOOR OF MERCY FOR ME. IN YOU PRECIOUS HOLY SPIRIT, I CAN SHOW MERCY IN ALL THINGS THAT GLORIFY MY HEAVENLY FATHER. I GIVE YOU THANKS PRECIOUS HOLY SPIRIT IN THE MIGHTY NAME OF JESUS. AMEN AND AMEN.

JUST A GLIMSE

OH LORD YOU HAVE GIVEN ME AN OUNCE OF WHAT YOU HAVE IN STORE FOR ME. PLEASE OPEN MINE EYES SO I CAN SEE.

OH LORD YOU HAVE GIVEN ME A GLIMSE OF YOUR ETERNAL GLORY. PLEASE HELP ME TO SHARE YOUR SALVATION'S STORY.

OH LORD YOU HAVE GIVEN ME A TASTE OF YOUR EVERLASTING GRACE. PLEASE HOLD ME IN YOUR WARM EMBRACE.

OH LORD YOU HAVE GIVEN ME A TOUCH OF YOUR AWESOME POWER. PLEASE HELP ME TO SAVOUR IT EACH AND EVERY HOUR.

OH LORD YOU HAVE GIVEN ME AN INCH OF YOUR ETERNAL LOVE. PLEASE SHOWER ME WITH BLESSINGS FROM YOUR STOREHOUSE ABOVE.

OH LORD YOU HAVE GIVEN ME A PEEK OF YOUR ETERNAL CITY. PLEASE HELP ME TO ENTER IT, I BEG YOUR PITY.

OH LORD YOU HAVE GIVEN ME A SECOND OF YOUR ETERNAL TIME. PLEASE MAKE ME YOURS FOR YOU ARE MINE.

HEAVENLY FATHER YOU ARE GOOD TO ME. PRECIOUS JESUS YOU ARE GOOD TO ME. PRECIOUS HOLY SPIRIT YOU ARE GOOD TO ME. HOLY TRINITY I APPRECIATE YOUR GOODNESS TOWARDS ME. I SAY THIS IN THE MIGHTY NAME OF JESUS. AMEN AND AMEN.

YOU HAVE A PLAN FOR ME PRECIOUS HOLY SPIRIT

YOU HAVE A PLAN FOR ME PRECIOUS HOLY SPIRIT. PLEASE LEAD ME BY YOUR HAND SO I CAN FULFILL YOUR ETERNAL PLAN.

YOU HAVE A PLAN FOR ME PRECIOUS HOLY SPIRIT. PLEASE LEAD ME EACH SECOND, TO YOU MY HEART DOES BECKON.

YOU HAVE A PLAN FOR ME PRECIOUS HOLY SPIRIT. PLEASE LEAD ME EACH MINUTE BY YOUR PLAN AS I CONTINUE IN IT.

YOU HAVE A PLAN FOR ME PRECIOUS HOLY SPIRIT. PLEASE LEAD ME EACH AND EVERY HOUR AS I DEPEND ON YOUR ETERNAL POWER.

YOU HAVE A PLAN FOR ME PRECIOUS HOLY SPIRIT. PLEASE LEAD ME EACH AND EVERY DAY AS I ACKNOWLEDGE THE ETERNAL PRICE CHRIST DID PAY.

YOU HAVE A PLAN FOR ME PRECIOUS HOLY SPIRIT. PLEASE LEAD ME EACH AND EVERY MONTH AS I SPEAK YOUR ETERNAL WORD SO BLUNT.

YOU HAVE A PLAN FOR ME PRECIOUS HOLY SPIRIT. PLEASE LEAD ME EACH AND EVERY YEAR BECAUSE MY HEART KNOWS HOW MUCH YOU CARE.

PLEASE TEACH ME YOUR PLAN, PRECIOUS HOLY SPIRIT. PLEASE LEAD ME AND GUIDE ME IN THE WAY IN WHICH I SHOULD GO. SPIRIT OF THE LIVING GOD, PLEASE TEACH ME TO DEPEND ON YOU AND HELP MY HEART TO CLING ONLY UNTO YOU. I PRAY THIS IN THE MIGHTY NAME OF JESUS. AMEN AND AMEN.

SET MY AFFAIRS IN ORDER PRECIOUS HOLY SPIRIT

SET MY AFFAIRS IN ORDER PRECIOUS HOLY SPIRIT. LET JESUS TAKE PRECEDENCE AT HOME IN MY RESIDENCE.

SET MY AFFAIRS IN ORDER PRECIOUS HOLY SPIRIT. LET JESUS LEAD THE WAY AS HE SHOWS ME THE WORDS I SHOULD SAY.

SET MY AFFAIRS IN ORDER PRECIOUS HOLY SPIRIT. LET JESUS DWELL IN MY HEART RIGHT FROM THE VERY START.

SET MY AFFAIRS IN ORDER PRECIOUS HOLY SPIRIT. LET JESUS TEACH ME TODAY AND HELP ME NEVER TO SWAY.

SET MY AFFAIRS IN ORDER PRECIOUS HOLY SPIRIT. LET JESUS OPEN MY HEART AND MAY HE NEVER DEPART.

SET MY AFFAIRS IN ORDER PRECIOUS HOLY SPIRIT. LET JESUS HOLD MY HAND AND REVEAL TO ME HIS WONDERFUL PLAN.

SET MY AFFAIRS IN ORDER PRECIOUS HOLY SPIRIT. LET JESUS HAVE HIS WAY, TODAY AND FOREVER I PRAY.

PRECIOUS HOLY SPIRIT PLEASE SET MY AFFAIRS IN ORDER. PROVOKE MY HEART, MY MIND AND MY SOUL PRECIOUS HOLY SPIRIT. PLEASE USE ME PRECIOUS HOLY SPIRIT TO GLORIFY THE FATHER, TO GLORIFY THE SON AND TO GLORIFY YOU PRECIOUS HOLY SPIRIT. I PRAY THIS IN THE MIGHTY NAME OF JESUS. AMEN AND AMEN.

PRECIOUS HOLY SPIRIT PLEASE BE WITH ME

SPIRIT OF THE LIVING GOD, PLEASE LET ME GO WHERE YOU GO.

SPIRIT OF THE LIVING GOD, PLEASE LET ME LAY WHERE YOU LAY.

SPIRIT OF THE LIVING GOD, PLEASE LET ME HOPE LIKE YOU HOPE.

SPIRIT OF THE LIVING GOD, PLEASE LET ME PRAY LIKE YOU PRAY.

SPIRIT OF THE LIVING GOD, PLEASE LET ME LIVE LIKE YOU LIVE.

SPIRIT OF THE LIVING GOD, PLEASE LET ME GIVE LIKE YOU GIVE.

SPIRIT OF THE LIVING GOD, PLEASE LET ME LOVE LIKE YOU LOVE.

SPIRIT OF THE LIVING GOD, PLEASE DO FOR ME WHAT I CANNOT DO FOR MYSELF. I NEED YOUR GUIDANCE PRECIOUS HOLY SPIRIT, I NEED YOUR WISDOM PRECIOUS HOLY SPIRIT AND I NEED YOUR LOVE PRECIOUS HOLY SPIRIT. I PRAY THIS IN THE MIGHT NAME OF JESUS. AMEN AND AMEN.

HAPPINESS IN YOUR PRESENCE
PRECIOUS HOLY SPIRIT

I AM THE HAPPIEST, WHEN I PARTAKE OF YOUR VERY BEST, PRECIOUS HOLY SPIRIT.

I HAVE PEACE OF MIND, WHEN I REPRESENT YOU TO ALL OF MANKIND, PRECIOUS HOLY SPIRIT.

I HAVE LOVE TO GIVE, WHEN I DARE TO LIVE, AS YOU WOULD HAVE ME TO LIVE, PRECIOUS HOLY SPIRIT.

I HAVE JOY DEVINE, WHEN I CAN RECLINE IN YOUR PRESENCE, PRECIOUS HOLY SPIRIT.

I HAVE HOPE IN YOU, WHEN I DARE TO DO THE THINGS YOU ASK ME TO, PRECIOUS HOLY SPIRIT.

I HAVE A GIFT TO GIVE, WHEN I DARE TO LIVE THE LIFE THAT YOU GIVE, PRECIOUS HOLY SPIRIT.

I HAVE ALL TO GAIN, WITHOUT ANY PAIN BECAUSE OF YOU, PRECIOUS HOLY SPIRIT.

SPIRIT OF THE LIVING GOD, I HUNGER FOR YOU. SPIRIT OF THE LIVING GOD, I THIRST FOR YOU. SPIRIT OF THE LIVING GOD, MY HEART YEARNS FOR YOU. SPIRIT OF THE LIVING GOD, PLEASE TAKE YOUR RIGHTFUL PLACE IN MY LIFE. I PRAY THIS IN THE PRECIOUS NAME OF JESUS. AMEN AND AMEN.

I DON'T WANT

I DON'T WANT A LIFE OF SIN, I WANT THE PRECIOUS HOLY SPIRIT TO DWELL WITHIN.

I DON'T WANT A LIFE OF PAIN, I WANT THE PRECIOUS HOLY SPIRIT TO HELP TIME AND TIME AGAIN.

I DON'T WANT A LIFE OF DOUBT, I WANT THE PRECIOUS HOLY SPIRIT TO SHOW ME WHAT MY HOLY FATHER IS ALL ABOUT.

I DON'T WANT A LIFE OF FEAR, I WANT THE PRECIOUS HOLY SPIRIT TO SHOW ME HOW MUCH HE CARES.

I DON'T WANT A LIFE OF TROUBLE, I WANT THE PRECIOUS HOLY SPIRIT TO PROTECT ME WITH HIS INCANDESCENT BUBBLE.

I DON'T WANT A LIFE OF HATE, I WANT THE PRECIOUS HOLY SPIRIT TO TEACH ME HOW TO APPRECIATE.

I DON'T WANT A LIVE OF ILL WILL, I WANT THE PRECIOUS HOLY SPIRIT TO SHOW ME MY HOLY FATHER'S GOOD WILL.

I THANK YOU PRECIOUS HOLY SPIRIT FOR TOUCHING MY HEART AND IMPARTING TO ME WORDS OF WISDOM. I THANK YOU SPIRIT OF THE LIVING GOD FOR ALLOWING ME TO BE USED BY YOU. PLEASE HAVE YOUR WAY IN MY LIFE PRECIOUS HOLY SPIRIT. I PRAY THIS IN THE MIGHTY NAME OF JESUS. AMEN AND AMEN.

I HAVE YOU PRECIOUS HOLY SPIRIT

WHEN I SEEM TO LOSE ALL HOPE AND I STRUGGLE TO COPE, I HAVE YOU PRECIOUS HOLY SPIRIT.

WHEN I TURN FROM YOU AND STRUGGLE TO KNOW WHAT TO DO, I HAVE YOU PRECIOUS HOLY SPIRIT.

WHEN I LOOK WITHIN AND MY LIGHT HAS BECOME DIM, I HAVE YOU PRECIOUS HOLY SPIRIT.

WHEN I TURN FROM YOUR WAY AND BEGIN TO STRAY, I HAVE YOU PRECIOUS HOLY SPIRIT.

WHEN I HURT INSIDE AND I STRUGGLE TO TAKE A STRIDE, I HAVE YOU PRECIOUS HOLY SPIRIT.

WHEN I HAVE RUN THE RACE AND I HAVE RECEIVED OF YOUR GRACE, I HAVE YOU PRECIOUS HOLY SPIRIT.

WHEN I SEEK YOUR PEACE AND LONG TO LAY BENEATH YOUR FLEECE, I HAVE YOU PRECIOUS HOLY SPIRIT.

PRECIOUS HOLY SPIRIT, I KNOW THAT I HAVE YOU NO MATTER THE CIRCUMSTANCE. YOUR LOVE FOR ME IS EVERLASTING AND MY SPIRIT KNOWS THAT VERY WELL. PLEASE REMIND ME FROM DAY TO DAY, AS I WALK IN YOUR PERFECT WAY, THAT I HAVE YOU PRECIOUS HOLY SPIRIT. AMEN AND AMEN.

IF WE DON'T

IF WE DON'T ABIDE IN YOUR PERFECT WILL, ALL WE GET IS MISERY AND ILL WILL.

IF WE DON'T WALK DAILY BY YOUR SIDE, ALL WE WILL DO IS TO SLIP AND WE WILL SURELY SLIDE.

IF WE DON'T LOOK TO YOU FOR COVER, YOUR HOLY SPIRIT OVER US DOESN'T HOVER.

IF WE DON'T LOOK TO YOU FOR GRACE, WE SURELY CANNOT ENDURE THE ROUGH COURSE OF THE RACE.

IF WE DON'T LOOK TO YOU TO BLESS, ALL WE GET IS LESS AND LESS AND LESS.

IF WE DON'T LOOK TO YOU FOR LOVE, WE CAN'T HAVE YOUR BLESSINGS FROM ABOVE.

IF WE DON'T LOOK TO YOU THIS DAY, WE NEGATE THE ETERNAL PRICE YOU DID PAY.

SPIRIT OF THE LIVING GOD, PLEASE TEACH US HOW TO LOOK TO JESUS. JESUS YOU ARE THE WORTHY PRIZE. HELP US TO MAKE YOU OUR FIRST LOVE. I PRAY THIS IN THE ETERNAL POWER OF YOUR NAME. AMEN AND AMEN.

I LIKE THE SOUND OF YOUR HEART BEAT PRECIOUS HOLY SPIRIT

I LIKE THE SOUND OF YOUR HEART BEAT PRECIOUS HOLY SPIRIT, IT REMINDS ME OF SOMETHING THAT IS EVER SO SWEET.

I LIKE THE SOUND OF YOUR HEART BEAT PRECIOUS HOLY SPIRIT, IT BEATS WITH KINDNESS, EACH BEAT CASCADES ALL YOUR GOODNESS.

I LIKE THE SOUND OF YOUR HEART BEAT PRECIOUS HOLY SPIRIT, WITH EACH BEAT I HEAR YOU SAY HOW MUCH YOU CARE.

I LIKE THE SOUND OF YOUR HEART BEAT PRECIOUS HOLY SPIRIT, WITH EACH BEAT I HEAR TENDERNESS, WITH EACH BEAT MY SOUL DRAWS NEAR.

I LIKE THE SOUND OF YOUR HEART BEAT PRECIOUS HOLY SPIRIT, MY EAR IS ATTENTIVE TO EACH BEAT AND IN YOU, I FIND SWEET RETREAT.

I LIKE THE SOUND OF YOUR HEART BEAT PRECIOUS HOLY SPIRIT, MY SPIRIT IS ATTENTIVE TO EACH BEAT AND WITH YOU, I CAN ACCOMPLISH ANY FEAT.

I LIKE THE SOUND OF YOUR HEART BEAT PRECIOUS HOLY SPIRIT, WITH EACH BEAT, I FALL IN LOVE AND MY SOUL IS SATISFIED FROM HEAVEN ABOVE.

PRECIOUS HOLY SPIRIT, PLEASE TEACH ME TO BE ATTENTIVE TO THE SOUND OF YOUR HEART BEAT. YOUR HEART BEAT GIVES ME LIFE, YOUR HEART BEAT GIVES ME STRENGTH AND YOUR HEART BEAT GIVES ME HOPE. I PRAY PRECIOUS HOLY SPIRIT THAT MY HEART BEAT WILL BE IN TUNE WITH YOUR HEART BEAT. THIS IS MY DESIRE. AMEN AND AMEN.

MOVE WITHIN ME PRECIOUS HOLY SPIRIT

MOVE WITHIN ME PRECIOUS HOLY SPIRIT, SO I CAN DO THE THINGS THAT ARE PLEASING TO YOU, PRECIOUS HOLY SPIRIT.

MOVE WITHIN ME PRECIOUS HOLY SPIRIT, SO I CAN LIVE A LIFE THAT IS PLEASING TO YOU, PRECIOUS HOLY SPIRIT.

MOVE WITHIN ME PRECIOUS HOLY SPIRIT, SO I CAN DO THE WORK THAT IS PLEASING TO YOU, PRECIOUS HOLY SPIRIT.

MOVE WITHIN ME PRECIOUS HOLY SPIRIT, SO I CAN GIVE THE LOVE THAT IS PLEASING TO YOU, PRECIOUS HOLY SPIRIT.

MOVE WITHIN ME PRECIOUS HOLY SPIRIT, SO I CAN SHARE THE MESSAGE THAT IS PLEASING TO YOU, PRECIOUS HOLY SPIRIT.

MOVE WITHIN ME PRECIOUS HOLY SPIRIT, SO I CAN BE A BLESSING THAT IS PLEASING TO YOU, PRECIOUS HOLY SPIRIT.

MOVE WITHIN ME PRECIOUS HOLY SPIRIT, SO I CAN ACCOMPLISH ALL THAT IS PLEASING TO YOU, PRECIOUS HOLY SPIRIT.

SPIRIT OF THE LIVING GOD, BREATHE UPON ME. SPIRIT OF THE LIVING GOD MAKE ME WHAT YOU WANT ME TO BE. SPIRIT OF THE LIVING GOD DWELL WITHIN ME. THIS IS MY PRAYER IN THE PRECIOUS NAME OF JESUS. AMEN AND AMEN.

PRECIOUS HOLY SPIRIT PLEASE TEACH ME HOW TO PRAY

PRECIOUS HOLY SPIRIT PLEASE TEACH ME HOW TO PRAY, PLEASE TEACH ME HOW TO PRAY IN YOUR ETERNAL WAY.

PRECIOUS HOLY SPIRIT PLEASE TEACH ME HOW TO PRAY, PLEASE WHISPER IN MY EAR THE WORDS I SHOULD SHARE.

PRECIOUS HOLY SPIRIT PLEASE TEACH ME HOW TO PRAY, PLEASE MOVE WITHIN MY HEART THE WORDS I MUST IMPART.

PRECIOUS HOLY SPIRIT PLEASE TEACH ME HOW TO PRAY, PLEASE IMPRESS WITHIN MY THOUGHTS, THE THINGS THAT WILL NEVER DEPART.

PRECIOUS HOLY SPIRIT PLEASE TEACH ME HOW TO PRAY, PLEASE ALLOW MY HEART TO SHARE AS I TELL THE WORLD HOW MUCH YOU CARE.

PRECIOUS HOLY SPIRIT PLEASE TEACH ME HOW TO PRAY, PLEASE INSPIRE ME EACH HOUR AS YOU DEMONSTRATE YOUR AWESOME POWER.

PRECIOUS HOLY SPIRIT PLEASE TEACH ME HOW TO PRAY, PLEASE ALLOW ME TO BE RECEPTIVE TO MY HOLY FATHERS' PERSPECTIVE.

PRECIOUS HOLY SPIRIT PLEASE TEACH ME HOW TO PRAY LIKE JESUS PRAYED. PLEASE TEACH ME HOW TO PRAY WITH POWER FROM THE THROWN OF OUR HEAVENLY FATHER. PLEASE TEACH ME HOW TO PRAY PRECIOUS HOLY SPIRIT, THE PRAYERS THAT WINS SOULS FOR OUR FATHERS' ETERNAL KINGDOM. THIS IS MY REQUEST IN JESUS MOST PRECIOUS NAME. AMEN AND AMEN.

I SURRENDER PRECIOUS HOLY SPIRIT

I SURRENDER PRECIOUS HOLY SPIRIT, I GIVE UP, PLEASE COME AND LIFT ME UP.

I SURRENDER PRECIOUS HOLY SPIRIT, I GIVE IN, PLEASE COME AND DWELL WITHIN.

I SURRENDER PRECIOUS HOLY SPIRIT, I AM LETTING GO, PLEASE COME AND ALLOW ME TO GROW.

I SURRENDER PRECIOUS HOLY SPIRIT, I AM SAYING GOOD BYE, PLEASE COME AND SING ME YOUR SWEET LULLABY.

I SURRENDER PRECIOUS HOLY SPIRIT, I AM LOOKING TO YOU, PLEASE COME AND MAKE MY LIFE BRAND NEW.

I SURRENDER PRECIOUS HOLY SPIRIT, I AM KNEELING DOWN, PLEASE COME AND TAKE ME TO YOUR HOLY GROUND.

I SURRENDER PRECIOUS HOLY SPIRIT, I AM SHOUTING OUT, PLEASE HELP ME TO TELL THE WORLD WHAT OUR LORD JESUS IS ALL ABOUT.

PRECIOUS HOLY SPIRIT, I SURRENDER TO YOU. I PLACE MY LIFE IN YOUR HANDS, PLEASE ALLOW ME TO BE USED ACCORDING TO YOUR PLANS. I ACKNOWLEDGE YOU AS MY COMFORTER HOLY SPIRIT AND THE ONE WHO GUIDES ME INTO ALL TRUTHS. I SURRENDER TO YOU SPIRIT OF THE LIVING GOD NOW AND ALWAYS. I PRAY THIS IN THE PRECIOUS NAME OF JESUS. AMEN AND AMEN.

PLEASE TEACH ME PRECIOUS HOLY SPIRIT

PLEASE TEACH ME PRECIOUS HOLY SPIRIT ABOUT THE THINGS THAT ARE DARE TO MY HEAVENLY FATHER'S HEART. PLEASE TEACH ME PRECIOUS HOLY SPIRIT ABOUT THE THINGS THAT MANKIND CANNOT IMPART.

PLEASE TEACH ME PRECIOUS HOLY SPIRIT ABOUT THE THINGS THAT MY HEAVENLY FATHER REQUIRES. PLEASE TEACH ME PRECIOUS HOLY SPIRIT BECAUSE THIS IS MY HEART'S DESIRE.

PLEASE TEACH ME PRECIOUS HOLY SPIRIT ABOUT THE THINGS THAT MY HEAVENLY FATHER DELIGHTS IN. PLEASE TEACH ME PRECIOUS HOLY SPIRIT ABOUT THE PLAN THAT WASHED AWAY ALL OF MY SINS.

PLEASE TEACH ME PRECIOUS HOLY SPIRIT ABOUT THE THINGS THAT ARE PRECIOUS TO MY FATHER'S HEART. PLEASE TEACH ME PRECIOUS HOLY SPIRIT SO THAT MY SPIRIT WILL NEVER DEPART.

PLEASE TEACH ME PRECIOUS HOLY SPIRIT ABOUT THE THINGS THAT MY HEAVENLY FATHER LOVES. PLEASE TEACH ME PRECIOUS HOLY SPIRIT ABOUT THE THINGS HE CHERISHES FROM ABOVE.

PLEASE TEACH ME PRECIOUS HOLY SPIRIT ABOUT MY HEAVENLY FATHER'S MERCIES. PLEASE TEACH ME PRECIOUS HOLY SPIRIT BECAUSE FOR THIS MY SOUL IS EVER SO THIRSTY.

PLEASE TEACH ME PRECIOUS HOLY SPIRIT ABOUT MY HEAVENLY FATHER'S ETERNAL SACRIFICE. PLEASE TEACH ME PRECIOUS HOLY SPIRIT BECAUSE I WANT TO LIVE FOR MY LORD AND SAVIOUR JESUS CHRIST.

PRECIOUS HOLY SPIRIT, PLEASE TEACH ME THINGS THAT ARE NEAR AND DARE TO THE HEART OF MY HEAVENLY FATHER. JESUS PROMISED THAT YOU PRECIOUS HOLY SPIRIT WILL LEAD ME INTO ALL TRUTHS. I ACCEPT YOUR GUIDANCE PRECIOUS HOLY SPIRIT. IN JESUS MOST HOLY NAME, I PRAY. AMEN AND AMEN.

MY MASTER CALLS ME TO THE BATTLEFIELD

MY MASTER CALLS ME TO THE BATTLEFIELD AND I WILL ANSWER. MY MASTER CALLS ME TO THE BATTLEFIELD AND I AM PREPARED TO GO WITH MY LANCER.

MY MASTER CALLS ME TO THE BATTLEFIELD AS THE SOLDIERS ALIGN. MY MASTER CALLS ME TO THE BATTLEFIELD, HE HAS PLACED ON ME HIS PRECIOUS SIGN.

MY MASTER CALLS ME TO THE BATTLEFIELD AND I WILL TAKE MY PLACE. MY MASTER CALLS ME TO THE BATTLEFIELD, HE HAS ADDRESSED ME FACE TO FACE.

MY MASTER CALLS ME TO THE BATTLEFIELD AND I AM PREPARED TO GO. MY MASTER CALLS ME TO THE BATTLEFIELD, HE PROMISED TO PROTECT ME, THIS I KNOW.

MY MASTER CALLS ME TO THE BATTLEFIELD AND I WILL NOT HESITATE. MY MASTER CALLS ME TO THE BATTLEFIELD AND ON HIM ONLY WILL I MEDITATE.

MY MASTER CALLS ME TO THE BATTLEFIELD AS MY HEART BEATS LOUD. MY MASTER CALLS ME TO THE BATTLEFIELD AS HE TELLS ME HOW MUCH HE IS PROUD.

MY MASTER CALLS ME TO THE BATTLEFIELD AND I WILL ANSWER HIS CALL. MY MASTER CALLS ME TO THE BATTLEFIELD, HE WILL DEFEND ME AT ANY COST AT ALL.

I THANK YOU FOR CALLING ME TO THE BATTLEFIELD PRECIOUS JESUS. I THANK YOU FOR THE CONFIDENCE YOU HAVE PLACED ON ME. MY DESIRE IS TO FOLLOW YOUR LEAD MY MASTER; BECAUSE, I KNOW YOU WILL PROTECT ME FROM ALL DISASTER. I GIVE YOU PRAISE PRECIOUS JESUS, NOW AND ALWAYS. AMEN AND AMEN.

PRECIOUS HOLY SPIRIT PLEASE BRING ME INTO MY FATHER'S PRESENCE

AS I SIT IN SILENCE AND WAIT, MY HEART IS YEARNING FOR YOU PRECIOUS HOLY SPIRIT TO BRING ME INTO MY FATHER'S PRESENCE.

AS I SEE THE RISING SUN, MY HEART IS YEARNING FOR YOU PRECIOUS HOLY SPIRIT TO BRING ME INTO MY FATHER'S PRESENCE.

AS I READ THE HOLY BOOK, MY HEART IS YEARNING FOR YOU PRECIOUS HOLY SPIRIT TO BRING ME INTO MY FATHER'S PRESENCE.

AS I GET DOWN ON MY KNEES, MY HEART IS YEARNING FOR YOU PRECIOUS HOLY SPIRIT TO BRING ME INTO MY FATHER'S PRESENCE.

AS I GO OUT THE DOOR, MY HEART IS YEARNING FOR YOU PRECIOUS HOLY SPIRIT TO BRING ME INTO MY FATHER'S PRESENCE.

AS I GREET A SMILING FACE, MY HEART IS YEARNING FOR YOU PRECIOUS HOLY SPIRIT TO BRING ME INTO MY FATHER'S PRESENCE.

AS I JOURNEY THROUGHOUT THE DAY, MY HEART IS YEARNING FOR YOU PRECIOUS HOLY SPIRIT, PLEASE BRING ME INTO MY FATHER'S PRESENCE.

PRECIOUS HOLY SPIRIT YOU ARE MY COMFORTER. AS YOU DID COMFORT OUR LORD AND SAVIOUR JESUS CHRIST, PLEASE COMFORT ME. AS YOUR PRESENCE SURROUNDED MY PRECIOUS JESUS, PLEASE SURROUND ME AND BRING ME INTO THE PRESENCE OF MY FATHER. I ASK THIS IN THE PRECIOUS NAME OF JESUS. AMEN AND AMEN.

PRECIOUS HOLY SPIRIT, I LOVE BEING IN YOUR PRESENCE

IN THE EARLY MORNING, I FEEL YOUR PRESENCE ADORNING AND I WILL TELL YOU, PRECIOUS HOLY SPIRIT, I LOVE BEING IN YOUR PRESENCE.

IN MY THOUGHTS, I FEEL YOUR PRESENCE FLOW AS YOU HELP ME TO GROW AND I WILL TELL YOU, PRECIOUS HOLY SPIRIT, I LOVE BEING IN YOUR PRESENCE.

IN THE MID DAY SUN, YOU ALLOW ME TO HAVE SOME FUN AND I WILL TELL YOU, PRECIOUS HOLY SPIRIT, I LOVE BEING IN YOUR PRESENCE.

IN THE COURSE OF MY DAY, I CAN FEEL YOUR SWAY AND I WILL TELL YOU, PRECIOUS HOLY SPIRIT, I LOVE BEING IN YOUR PRESENCE.

IN THE TWILIGHT ZONE, YOU MAKE YOUR PRESENCE KNOWN AND I WILL TELL YOU, PRECIOUS HOLY SPIRIT, I LOVE BEING IN YOUR PRESENCE.

IN THE MIDDLE OF THE NIGHT AS YOU HOLD ME TIGHT AND I WILL TELL YOU, PRECIOUS HOLY SPIRIT, I LOVE BEING IN YOUR PRESENCE.

IN ALL THAT I DO, I AM GLAD YOU STICK TO ME LIKE GLUE AND I WILL TELL YOU, PRECIOUS HOLY SPIRIT, I LOVE BEING IN YOUR PRESENCE.

I THANK YOU FOR YOUR PRESENCE HOLY SPIRIT. YOUR PRESENCE IS SO SWEET AND SO REFRESHING, I DO NOT WANT A MOMENT TO GO BY WITHOUT YOU BY MY SIDE AND I WILL TELL YOU, PRECIOUS HOLY SPIRIT, I LOVE BEING IN YOUR PRESENCE. I THANK YOU PRECIOUS HOLY SPIRIT IN THE PRECIOUS NAME OF JESUS. AMEN AND AMEN.

I AM LETTING GO PRECIOUS HOLY SPIRIT

I AM LETTING GO SO I CAN FALL INTO YOUR ARMS. I AM LETTING GO SO I CAN ENJOY ALL OF YOUR CHARMS.

I AM LETTING GO OF MY SINFUL WAYS. I AM LETTING GO SO YOU CAN DIRECT ME FOR THE REST OF MY DAYS.

I AM LETTING GO OF ALL MY SHAME. I AM LETTING GO AND HOLDING ONTO JESUS NAME.

I AM LETTING GO OF WHAT I CONTROL. I AM LETTING GO SO SALVATION STORY CAN BE TOLD.

I AM LETTING GO OF ALL THAT IS WRONG. I AM LETTING GO SO YOU CAN MAKE ME STRONG.

I AM LETTING GO OF ALL MY FEARS. I AM LETTING GO SO YOU CAN DRY MY TEARS.

I AM LETTING GO OF ALL THAT FLACK. I AM LETTING GO AND NEVER LOOKING BACK.

PRECIOUS HOLY SPIRIT, I AM LETTING GO SO I CAN BE SECURE IN YOUR ARMS AND BE SURROUNDED BY ALL OF YOUR CHARMS. IN YOUR ARMS, I AM COMFORTED HOLY SPIRIT AND MY SOUL CAN HAVE SOME PEACE AND REST. I THANK YOU PRECIOUS JESUS FOR SENDING ME YOUR HOLY SPIRIT. I ACCEPT YOU PRECIOUS HOLY SPIRIT IN THE NAME OF JESUS. AMEN AND AMEN.

PLEASE TEACH ME HOW TO PRAY PRECIOUS HOLY SPIRIT LIKE JESUS PRAYED

PLEASE TEACH ME HOW TO PRAY PRECIOUS HOLY SPIRIT LIKE JESUS PRAYED. MY PRECIOUS JESUS SAID "OUR FATHER WHO IS IN HEAVEN HOLY IS YOUR NAME." PLEASE TEACH ME PRECIOUS HOLY SPIRIT TO DO THE SAME.

PLEASE TEACH ME HOW TO PRAY PRECIOUS HOLY SPIRIT LIKE JESUS PRAYED. MY PRECIOUS JESUS SAID "LET THY KINGDOM COME AND LET THY WILL BE DONE HERE ON EARTH AS IT IS IN HEAVEN." PLEASE TEACH ME PRECIOUS HOLY SPIRIT TO DO THE SAME.

PLEASE TEACH ME HOW TO PRAY PRECIOUS HOLY SPIRIT LIKE JESUS PRAYED. MY PRECIOUS JESUS SAID "GIVE US THIS DAY OUR DAILY BREAD." PLEASE TEACH ME PRECIOUS HOLY SPIRIT TO DO THE SAME.

PLEASE TEACH ME HOW TO PRAY PRECIOUS HOLY SPIRIT LIKE JESUS PRAYED. MY PRECIOUS JESUS SAID "AND FORGIVE US OUR TRESPASS AS WE FORGIVE THOSE WHO TRESPASS AGAINST US." PLEASE TEACH ME PRECIOUS HOLY SPIRIT TO DO THE SAME.

PLEASE TEACH ME HOW TO PRAY PRECIOUS HOLY SPIRIT LIKE JESUS PRAYED. MY PRECIOUS JESUS SAID "AND LEAD US NOT INTO TEMPTATION BUT DELIVER US FROM EVIL." PLEASE TEACH ME PRECIOUS HOLY SPIRIT TO DO THE SAME.

PLEASE TEACH ME HOW TO PRAY PRECIOUS HOLY SPIRIT LIKE JESUS PRAYED. MY PRECIOUS JESUS SAID "FOR THINE IS THE KINGDOM." PLEASE TEACH ME PRECIOUS HOLY SPIRIT TO DO THE SAME.

PLEASE TEACH ME HOW TO PRAY PRECIOUS HOLY SPIRIT LIKE JESUS PRAYED. MY PRECIOUS JESUS SAID "AND THE POWER AND THE GLORY FOREVER AND EVER AMEN." PLEASE TEACH ME PRECIOUS HOLY SPIRIT TO DO THE SAME.

IT IS OFTEN SAID THAT MIMICRY IS THE GREATEST FORM OF FLATTERY. IF THAT IS THE CASE, I WANT YOU PRECIOUS HOLY SPIRIT TO HELP ME TO MIMICK MY PRECIOUS JESUS IN EVERY WAY. I MAKE THIS PETITION IN THE PRECIOUS NAME OF JESUS. AMEN AND AMEN.

PLEASE TEACH ME HOW TO HEAL LIKE JESUS HEALED PRECIOUS HOLY SPIRIT

PLEASE TEACH ME HOW TO OPEN THE EYES OF THE BLIND, LIKE JESUS OPENED THE EYES OF THE BLIND PRECIOUS HOLY SPIRIT.

PLEASE TEACH ME HOW TO OPEN THE EARS OF THE DEAF, LIKE JESUS OPENED THE EARS OF THE DEAF PRECIOUS HOLY SPIRIT.

PLEASE TEACH ME HOW TO LOOSEN THE TONGUE OF THE MUTE, LIKE JESUS LOOSEN THE TONGUE OF THE MUTE PRECIOUS HOLY SPIRIT.

PLEASE TEACH ME HOW TO MAKE THE LAME WALK, LIKE JESUS MADE THE LAME WALK PRECIOUS HOLY SPIRIT.

PLEASE TEACH ME HOW TO CAST OUT DEMONS, LIKE JESUS CAST OUT DEMONS PRECIOUS HOLY SPIRIT.

PLEASE TEACH ME HOW TO RAISE THE DEAD, LIKE JESUS RAISED THE DEAD PRECIOUS HOLY SPIRIT.

PLEASE TEACH ME HOW TO CARE, LIKE OUR PRECIOUS LORD AND SAVIOUR JESUS CHRIST CARES PRECIOUS HOLY SPIRIT.

PRECIOUS HOLY FATHER, I COME TO YOU BY THE PROMPTING OF YOUR HOLY SPIRIT. I AM ASKING YOU HOLY FATHER IN THE MIGHTY NAME OF JESUS FOR YOUR HELP IN MY WALK IN THIS LIFE. PRECIOUS HOLY FATHER, I WANT TO BE LIKE YOUR PRECIOUS SON JESUS. PRECIOUS HOLY FATHER, I WANT TO DO YOUR PERFECT WILL. I PRAY THIS IN THE WONDERFUL NAME OF JESUS. AMEN AND AMEN.

BRING "IT" PRECIOUS HOLY SPIRIT

PLEASE BRING YOUR PEACE WHERE THERE IS DESPAIR. PLEASE BRING "IT" PRECIOUS HOLY SPIRIT I PRAY.

PLEASE BRING YOUR JOY TO REPLACE WHAT THE ENEMY DID DESTROY. PLEASE BRING "IT" PRECIOUS HOLY SPIRIT I PRAY.

PLEASE BRING YOUR HOPE SO WE CAN BROADEN OUR SCOPE. PLEASE BRING "IT" PRECIOUS HOLY SPIRIT I PRAY.

PLEASE BRING YOUR WEALTH AND YOUR PERFECT HEALTH TO OUR HEARTS. PLEASE BRING "IT" PRECIOUS HOLY SPIRIT I PRAY.

PLEASE BRING YOUR WISDOM AND ALL OF US TO BUILD YOUR KINGDOM. PLEASE BRING "IT" PRECIOUS HOLY SPIRIT I PRAY.

PLEASE BRING YOUR TRUTH AND ESTABLISH IT IN OUR YOUTH. PLEASE BRING "IT" PRECIOUS HOLY SPIRIT I PRAY.

PLEASE BRING YOUR LOVE FROM OUR HOLY FATHER FROM ABOVE. PLEASE BRING "IT" PRECIOUS HOLY SPIRIT I PRAY.

PRECIOUS HOLY SPIRIT, MY PRECIOUS SAVIOUR SAID, YOU WILL BE OUR COMFORTER; YOU WILL BE OUR GUIDE AND YOU WILL LEAD US INTO ALL TRUTH. PLEASE COME AND FULFILL OUR HEAVENLY FATHER'S WILL IN US, PRECIOUS HOLY SPIRIT I PRAY. THIS IS MY PRAYER IN JESUS PRECIOUS NAME. AMEN AND AMEN.

HELP ME PRECIOUS HOLY SPIRIT I PRAY

WHEN I AM TEMPTED TO DO WRONG AND THE DESIRE IS SO STRONG, PLEASE HELP ME PRECIOUS HOLY SPIRIT I PRAY.

WHEN TEMPTED TO BE DECEPTIVE AND MY HEART IS NOT RECEPTIVE, PLEASE HELP ME PRECIOUS HOLY SPIRIT I PRAY.

WHEN THE THOUGHTS ARE IN MY HEAD TO GIVE UP ON WHAT YOU SAID, PLEASE HELP ME PRECIOUS HOLY SPIRIT I PRAY.

WHEN THE DANGER IS SO CLOSE AND I CAN SMELL IT LIKE BURNT TOAST, PLEASE HELP ME PRECIOUS HOLY SPIRIT I PRAY.

WHEN I GAZE UPON TEMPTATION'S LURE AND I AM NOT FEELING SO SURE, PLEASE HELP ME PRECIOUS HOLY SPIRIT I PRAY.

WHEN I AM VERY WEAK AND I DON'T HAVE A VOICE TO SPEAK, PLEASE HELP ME PRECIOUS HOLY SPIRIT I PRAY.

WHEN ALL IS SAID AND DONE AND I AM SITTING AT THE BOTTOM WRONG, I WILL SAY, PLEASE HELP ME PRECIOUS HOLY SPIRIT I PRAY.

PRECIOUS HOLY SPIRIT, I AM CALLING OUT TO YOU TO HELP ME FOLLOW THROUGH TO DO THE THINGS THAT ARE PLEASING TO YOU. PLEASE HEIGHTEN MY SENSES AND HELP ME NOT TO SIT ON THE FENCES. PLEASE MAKE ME BRAND NEW AND HELP ME TO STAND ETERNALLY FOR YOU. I ASK THIS IN THE PRECIOUS NAME OF JESUS. AMEN AND AMEN.

WHEN I PRAY PRECIOUS HOLY SPIRIT

WHEN I PRAY, YOU TALK AND I LISTEN. THEN YOU TELL ME WHAT I HAVE BEEN MISSING PRECIOUS HOLY SPIRIT.

WHEN I PRAY, YOU TALK AND I HEAR. THEN YOU TELL ME HOW MUCH YOU CARE PRECIOUS HOLY SPIRIT.

WHEN I PRAY, YOU TALK AND I FEEL. THEN YOU TELL ME YOUR LOVE IS FOR REAL PRECIOUS HOLY SPIRIT.

WHEN I PRAY, YOU TALK AND I SEE. THEN YOU TELL ME HOW LIFE SHOULD BE PRECIOUS HOLY SPIRIT.

WHEN I PRAY, YOU TALK AND I TOUCH. THEN YOU TELL ME, YOU LOVE ME SO VERY MUCH PRECIOUS HOLY SPIRIT.

WHEN I PRAY, YOU TALK AND I REACH. THEN YOU TELL ME HOW I SHOULD TEACH PRECIOUS HOLY SPIRIT.

WHEN I PRAY, YOU TALK AND I SAY, THANK YOU FOR GUIDING ME INTO ALL TRUTH PRECIOUS HOLY SPIRIT.

PLEASE ALLOW ME TO POUR OUT MY HEART TO YOU WHEN I PRAY PRECIOUS HOLY SPIRIT. HELP ME TO COMMUNICATE WITH YOU THROUGHOUT THE DAY AND ALONG LIFE'S NARROW WAY. PLEASE GUIDE ME PRECIOUS HOLY SPIRIT I PRAY IN JESUS NAME. AMEN AND AMEN.

I RECEIVE OF YOUR BLESSINGS PRECIOUS HOLY SPIRIT

I RECEIVE OF YOUR BLESSINGS PRECIOUS HOLY SPIRIT, I RECEIVE IT EVERY YEAR AND I LIVE WITHOUT DESPAIR.

I RECEIVE OF YOUR BLESSINGS PRECIOUS HOLY SPIRIT, I RECEIVE IT EVERY MONTH AND YOU SATISFY ME WHEN I HUNT.

I RECEIVE OF YOUR BLESSINGS PRECIOUS HOLY SPIRIT, I RECEIVE IT EVERY DAY AND I AM SO GLAD YOU ARE HERE TO STAY.

I RECEIVE OF YOUR BLESSINGS PRECIOUS HOLY SPIRIT, I RECEIVE IT EVERY HOUR AND I AM FILLED WITH YOUR AWESOME POWER.

I RECEIVE OF YOUR BLESSINGS PRECIOUS HOLY SPIRIT, I RECEIVE IT EVERY MINUTE AND I AM SO GLAD THAT YOU ARE IN IT.

I RECEIVE OF YOUR BLESSINGS PRECIOUS HOLY SPIRIT, I RECEIVE IT EVERY SECOND, BECAUSE YOU ANSWER ME WHEN I BECKON.

I RECEIVE OF YOUR BLESSINGS PRECIOUS HOLY SPIRIT, I RECEIVE IN ALL SPACE AND TIME AND I AM SO GLAD THAT, YOU PRECIOUS JESUS, YOU ARE MINE.

I THANK YOU PRECIOUS HOLY SPIRIT FOR LEADING ME INTO ALL TRUTHS. I THANK YOU FOR BEING WITH ME IN EVERY SITUATION. I DEPEND UPON YOU SPIRIT OF THE LIVING GOD, JUST LIKE MY SAVIOUR JESUS DID. I THANK YOU IN THE MIGHTY NAME OF JESUS PRECIOUS HOLY SPIRIT. AMEN AND AMEN.

THANK YOU PRECIOUS HOLY SPIRIT

THANK YOU PRECIOUS HOLY SPIRIT FOR ALLOWING ME TO BE OBEDIENT, FOR ONLY THEN CAN I TRULY BE YOUR STUDENT.

THANK YOU PRECIOUS HOLY SPIRIT FOR ALLOWING ME TO BE ATTENTIVE, FOR ONLY THEN CAN YOUR WORK BE REDEMPTIVE.

THANK YOU PRECIOUS HOLY SPIRIT FOR ALLOWING ME TO BE STILL, FOR ONLY THEN CAN YOU PERFECT YOUR EVERLASTING WILL.

THANK YOU PRECIOUS HOLY SPIRIT FOR ALLOWING ME TO BE KIND, FOR ONLY THEN CAN YOU IMPART YOUR PERFECT MIND.

THANK YOU PRECIOUS HOLY SPIRIT FOR ALLOWING ME TO BE BOLD, FOR ONLY THEN CAN SALVATION'S STORY BE TOLD.

THANK YOU PRECIOUS HOLY SPIRIT FOR ALLOWING ME TO BE TRUE, FOR ONLY THEN CAN ALL THINGS BEGIN ANEW.

THANK YOU PRECIOUS HOLY SPIRIT FOR ALLOWING ME TO LOVE, FOR ONLY THEN CAN YOUR BLESSINGS FLOW FROM ABOVE.

I THANK YOU PRECIOUS HOLY SPIRIT FOR DOING YOUR ETERNAL WORK WITHIN ME. I APPRECIATE YOUR COMPANIONSHIP AND YOUR WARM EMBRACE. PLEASE NEVER LEAVE MY SIDE AND WITH YOU, I WILL ALWAYS ABIDE. I PRAY THIS IN THE PRECIOUS NAME OF JESUS. AMEN AND AMEN.

BE IN EVERY PART OF ME PRECIOUS HOLY SPIRIT I PRAY

BE IN EVERY PART OF ME PRECIOUS HOLY SPIRIT I PRAY, BE MY BREATH AND DELIVER ME FROM ETERNAL DEATH.

BE IN EVERY PART OF ME PRECIOUS HOLY SPIRIT I PRAY, BE MY HOPE AND BROADEN THE HORIZONS OF MY SCOPE.

BE IN EVERY PART OF ME PRECIOUS HOLY SPIRIT I PRAY, BE MY EYES AND INSTRUCT ME HOW TO BECOME WISE.

BE IN EVERY PART OF ME PRECIOUS HOLY SPIRIT I PRAY, BE MY MOUTH AND TEACH ME HOW TO SING OUT LOUD AND HOW TO SHOUT.

BE IN EVERY PART OF ME PRECIOUS HOLY SPIRIT I PRAY, BE MY HANDS AND TEACH ME OF YOUR ETERNAL PLANS.

BE IN EVERY PART OF ME PRECIOUS HOLY SPIRIT I PRAY, BE MY FEET AND PROTECT ME FROM DEFEAT.

BE IN EVERY PART OF ME PRECIOUS HOLY SPIRIT I PRAY, BE MY HEART AND FROM YOU I WILL NEVER DEPART.

PRECIOUS HOLY SPIRIT BE IN EVERY PART OF ME I PRAY. PLEASE DIRECT MY DAILY AFFAIRS AND LET ME NEVER BE IN ARREARS. PRECIOUS HOLY SPIRIT I PRAY, PLEASE TEACH ME HOW TO LISTEN TO AND ALLOW ME TO FOLLOW YOUR INSTRUCTIONS. I ASK THIS IN THE PRECIOUS NAME OF JESUS. AMEN AND AMEN.

PUT ALL THAT IS GOOD IN MY HEART PRECIOUS HOLY SPIRIT

PUT PEACE IN MY HEART PRECIOUS HOLY SPIRIT I PRAY. PUT IT IN TODAY, FOREVER AND ALWAYS.

PUT JOY IN MY HEART PRECIOUS HOLY SPIRIT I PRAY. PUT IT IN TODAY, FOREVER AND ALWAYS.

PUT HOPE IN MY HEART PRECIOUS HOLY SPIRIT I PRAY. PUT IT IN TODAY, FOREVER AND ALWAYS.

PUT PATIENCE IN MY HEART PRECIOUS HOLY SPIRIT I PRAY. PUT IT IN TODAY, FOREVER AND ALWAYS.

PUT GRACE IN MY HEART PRECIOUS HOLY SPIRIT I PRAY. PUT IT IN TODAY, FOREVER AND ALWAYS.

PUT MERCY IN MY HEART PRECIOUS HOLY SPIRIT I PRAY. PUT IT IN TODAY, FOREVER AND ALWAYS.

PUT LOVE IN MY HEART PRECIOUS HOLY SPIRIT I PRAY. PUT IT IN TODAY, FOREVER AND ALWAYS.

PRECIOUS HOLY SPIRIT I PRAY; PLEASE FILL MY HEART WITH ALL THAT IS GOOD, WITH ALL THAT IS PURE AND WITH ALL THAT IS HOLY. SPIRIT OF THE LIVING GOD, PLEASE TEACH MY HEART TO BE IN TUNE WITH YOUR HEART. I ASK THIS IN THE MIGHTY NAME OF JESUS. AMEN AND AMEN.

I HAVE MY FATHER'S WORK TO DO PRECIOUS HOLY SPIRIT

I HAVE MY FATHER'S WORK TO DO PRECIOUS HOLY SPIRIT. PLEASE GRANT ME YOUR WISDOM SO I CAN FILL YOUR ETERNAL KINGDOM.

I HAVE MY FATHER'S WORK TO DO PRECIOUS HOLY SPIRIT. PLEASE GRANT ME YOUR KNOWLEDGE AND YOU I WILL ALWAYS ACKNOWLEDGE.

I HAVE MY FATHER'S WORK TO DO PRECIOUS HOLY SPIRIT. PLEASE GRANT ME YOUR UNDERSTANDING AND HELP ME TO AVOID ALL THIS SLANDERING.

I HAVE MY FATHER'S WORK TO DO PRECIOUS HOLY SPIRIT. PLEASE GRANT ME YOUR MERCY AND BLESS ME WHEN I AM THIRSTY.

I HAVE MY FATHER'S WORK TO DO PRECIOUS HOLY SPIRIT. PLEASE GRANT ME YOUR GRACE AND HELP ME TO REFLECT JESUS' FACE.

I HAVE MY FATHER'S WORK TO DO PRECIOUS HOLY SPIRIT. PLEASE GRANT ME YOUR HOPE AND HELP ME TO BROADEN MY SCOPE.

I HAVE MY FATHER'S WORK TO DO PRECIOUS HOLY SPIRIT. PLEASE GRANT ME YOUR LOVE AND LET IT REST UPON ME WITH POWER FROM ABOVE.

PRECIOUS HOLY SPIRIT, I HAVE MY FATHER'S WORK TO DO. PLEASE HELP ME SO I CAN BRING GLORY AND HONOUR TO MY FATHER'S NAME. I ASK THIS IN THE MOST PRECIOUS NAME OF JESUS. AMEN AND AMEN.

BE MY VALENTINE PRECIOUS HOLY SPIRIT, I PRAY

BE MY VALENTINE PRECIOUS HOLY SPIRIT, I PRAY. BECAUSE YOU HAVE LOVED ME SO ENDLESSLY IN MY SINFUL WAY.

BE MY VALENTINE PRECIOUS HOLY SPIRIT, I PRAY. PLEASE OPEN MY HEART AND GRANT ME A BRAND NEW START.

BE MY VALENTINE PRECIOUS HOLY SPIRIT, I PRAY. PLEASE BLESS ME WITH YOUR TREASURES AND ENVELOPE ME WITH YOUR PLEASURES.

BE MY VALENTINE PRECIOUS HOLY SPIRIT, I PRAY. PLEASE HELP ME TO KNOW HOW MUCH YOU WANT ME TO GROW.

BE MY VALENTINE PRECIOUS HOLY SPIRIT, I PRAY. PLEASE HOLD MY HAND AND GENTLY LEAD ME IN YOUR PLAN.

BE MY VALENTINE PRECIOUS HOLY SPIRIT, I PRAY. PLEASE TAKE AWAY ALL MY DOUBTS AND PLEASE TELL ME WHAT YOU ARE ALL ABOUT.

BE MY VALENTINE PRECIOUS HOLY SPIRIT, I PRAY. PLEASE HELP ME TO APPRECIATE THE LOVE YOU INITIATE.

PRECIOUS HOLY SPIRIT, THIS IS MY APPRECIATION FOR THE PERFECT LOVE YOU HAVE LAVISHED ON ME. I THANK YOU PRECIOUS HOLY SPIRIT FOR YOUR UNFAILING LOVE. YOUR LOVE IS THE LOVE I DESIRE AND YOUR LOVE IS THE ONLY LOVE I REQUIRE. I THANK YOU FOR YOUR LOVE PRECIOUS HOLY SPIRIT, NOW AND ALWAYS. AMEN AND AMEN.

I WILL STEP ASIDE AND LET YOU LEAD PRECIOUS HOLY SPIRIT

I WILL STEP ASIDE AND LET YOU LEAD PRECIOUS HOLY SPIRIT, THIS MY PRAYER, THIS IS MY CREED.

I WILL STEP ASIDE AND LET YOU LEAD PRECIOUS HOLY SPIRIT, THIS IS WHAT IS IN MY HEART, PLEASE DON'T LET IT EVER DEPART.

I WILL STEP ASIDE AND LET YOU LEAD PRECIOUS HOLY SPIRIT, I WILL DEDICATE MY LIFE TO YOU, BECAUSE YOU GAVE YOUR PROMISE TO SEE ME THROUGH.

I WILL STEP ASIDE AND LET YOU LEAD PRECIOUS HOLY SPIRIT, I WILL LISTEN TO YOUR VOICE AND I WILL MAKE THAT MY FIRST CHOICE.

I WILL STEP ASIDE AND LET YOU LEAD PRECIOUS HOLY SPIRIT, I WILL DO MY BEST NOT TO COMPLAIN, BECAUSE YOU PROTECTED ME TIME AND TIME AGAIN.

I WILL STEP ASIDE AND LET YOU LEAD PRECIOUS HOLY SPIRIT, I WILL STICK CLOSE TO YOU AND PERFORM WHAT YOU ASK ME TO DO.

I WILL STEP ASIDE AND LET YOU LEAD PRECIOUS HOLY SPIRIT, I WILL GIVE YOU ALL OF MY PRAISE, FOR THE REST OF MY DAYS.

WHERE YOU LEAD, I WILL FOLLOW PRECIOUS HOLY SPIRIT. I GIVE MY HEART, MY MIND AND MY SOUL TO YOU. PLEASE USE ME TO DO MY HEAVENLY FATHER'S WIIL, WHILE I AM YIELDED AND STILL. I PRAY THIS IN THE MIGHTY NAME OF JESUS. AMEN AND AMEN.

I NEED YOUR SEAL OF APPROVAL PRECIOUS HOLY SPIRIT

PRECIOUS HOLY SPIRIT, I FEEL THE HUNGER TO DO MY HEAVENLY FATHER'S PERFECT WILL. I NEED YOUR SEAL OF APPROVAL PRECIOUS HOLY SPIRIT TO HELP ME THIS TO FULFILL.

PRECIOUS HOLY SPIRIT, I FEEL A THIRST FOR JESUS PRESENCE. I NEED YOUR SEAL OF APPROVAL PRECIOUS HOLY SPIRIT TO HELP ME WITH MY DEFIANCE.

PRECIOUS HOLY SPIRIT, I FEEL A NEED TO CALL OUT TO YOU. I NEED YOUR SEAL OF APPROVAL PRECIOUS HOLY SPIRIT SO I CAN DO THE THINGS YOU WANT ME TO DO.

PRECIOUS HOLY SPIRIT, I FEEL A BURDEN ON ME WHICH I CANNOT BARE ALONE. I NEED YOUR SEAL OF APPROVAL PRECIOUS HOLY SPIRIT SO MY PRECIOUS JESUS CAN ATONE.

PRECIOUS HOLY SPIRIT, I FEEL A FEAR THAT WANTS TO DRAW NEAR. I NEED YOUR SEAL OF APPROVAL PRECIOUS HOLY SPIRIT TO TELL THAT FOUL SPIRIT TO DISAPPEAR.

PRECIOUS HOLY SPIRIT, I FEEL A NEED TO GET DOWN ON MY KNEES. I NEED YOUR SEAL OF APPROVAL PRECIOUS HOLY SPIRIT SO I CAN DO YOUR ETERNAL WILL, IF YOU PLEASE.

PRECIOUS HOLY SPIRIT, I FEEL YOUR PRESENCE EVERYWHERE. I NEED YOUR SEAL OF APPROVAL PRECIOUS HOLY SPIRIT TO LIVE IN YOU WITHOUT DESPAIR.

I THANK YOU PRECIOUS JESUS FOR SENDING YOUR CHILDREN THE PRECIOUS HOLY COMFORTER, THE PRECIOUS HOLY SPIRIT. YOU HAVE PROMISED THAT WHEN HE COMES, HE WILL LEAD US INTO ALL TRUTHS. I AM CLAIMING YOUR PROMISE PRECIOUS JESUS. I NEED YOUR SEAL OF APPROVAL PRECIOUS HOLY SPIRIT TO DO MY HEAVENLY FATHER'S PERFECT WILL. I PRAY THIS IN THE MOST PRECIOUS NAME OF JESUS. AMEN AND AMEN.

I WILL GO WHERE YOU WANT ME TO GO PRECIOUS HOLY SPIRIT

PRECIOUS HOLY SPIRIT PLEASE LEAD ME INTO ALL TRUTHS. BECAUSE I AM WILLING, I AM WILLING TO GO WHERE YOU WANT ME TO GO PRECIOUS HOLY SPIRIT.

PRECIOUS HOLY SPIRIT PLEASE PLACE YOUR WORDS INTO MY MOUTH. BECAUSE I AM WILLING TO SAY WHAT YOU WANT ME TO SAY PRECIOUS HOLY SPIRIT.

PRECIOUS HOLY SPIRIT PLEASE BLESSS ME WITH YOUR ETERNAL BLESSINGS. BECAUSE I AM WILLING TO BLESS OTHERS AS YOU HAVE BLESSED ME PRECIOUS HOLY SPIRIT.

PRECIOUS HOLY SPIRIT PLEASE TEACH ME HOW TO PRAY LIKE JESUS PRAYED. BECAUSE I AM WILLING TO PRAY FOR OTHERS AS JESUS PRAYED FOR OTHERS PRECIOUS HOLY SPIRIT.

PRECIOUS HOLY SPIRIT PLEASE TEACH ME HOW TO GIVE LIKE JESUS GAVE. BECAUSE I AM WILLING TO GIVE TO OTHERS AS I HAVE BEEN GIVEN PRECIOUS HOLY SPIRIT.

PRECIOUS HOLY SPIRIT PLEASE TEACH ME HOW TO CARE LIKE JESUS CARES. BECAUSE I AM WILLING TO CARE FOR OTHERS AS I HAVE BEEN CARED FOR PRECIOUS HOLY SPIRIT.

PRECIOUS HOLY SPIRIT PLEASE TEACH ME HOW TO LOVE LIKE JESUS LOVED. BECAUSE I AM WILLING TO LOVE OTHERS AS PRECIOUS JESUS HAS LOVED ME PRECIOUS HOLY SPIRIT.

PRECIOUS HOLY SPIRIT, I AM RELYING ON YOU TO LEAD ME INTO ALL TRUTHS. PLEASE GIVE ME THE COURAGE, THE STRENGTH AND THE DETERMINATION TO FOLLOW YOUR LEAD PRECIOUS HOLY SPIRIT. I ASK THIS IN THE MOST PRECIOUS NAME OF JESUS. AMEN AND AMEN.

HELP ME PRECIOUS HOLY SPIRIT

HELP ME PRECIOUS HOLY SPIRIT TO LOVE MORE AND MORE LIKE JESUS.

HELP ME PRECIOUS HOLY SPIRIT TO GIVE MORE AND MORE LIKE JESUS.

HELP ME PRECIOUS HOLY SPIRIT TO BLESS MORE AND MORE LIKE JESUS.

HELP ME PRECIOUS HOLY SPIRIT TO PRAY MORE AND MORE LIKE JESUS.

HELP ME PRECIOUS HOLY SPIRIT TO PRAISE MORE AND MORE LIKE JESUS.

HELP ME PRECIOUS HOLY SPIRIT TO UNDERSTAND MORE AND MORE LIKE JESUS.

HELP ME PRECIOUS HOLY SPIRIT TO BE MORE AND MORE LIKE JESUS.

PRECIOUS SPIRIT OF THE LIVING GOD, PLEASE BREATHE UPON ME AND COME AND LIVE WITHIN ME. SPIRIT OF THE LIVING GOD, PLEASE SHOW ME THE HEART BEAT OF OUR FATHER WHO LIVES IN HEAVEN AND HELP ME TO GLORIFY HIS NAME, TIME AND TIME AGAIN. IN JESUS MOST PRECIOUS NAME, I PRAY. AMEN AND AMEN.

PRECIOUS HOLY SPIRIT I NEED TO KNOW YOU

PRECIOUS HOLY SPIRIT I NEED TO KNOW YOU. PLEASE TEACH ME ALL I NEED TO KNOW ABOUT YOU.

PRECIOUS HOLY SPIRIT I NEED TO SEE YOU. I NEED TO SEE ALL THE TRUTHS THERE IS TO KNOW ABOUT YOU.

PRECIOUS HOLY SPIRIT I NEED TO HEAR YOU. PLEASE WHISPER IN MY EAR THE THINGS THAT CAUSE ME TO PERFECTLY FEAR (RESPECT) YOU.

PRECIOUS HOLY SPIRIT I NEED TO TOUCH YOU. I NEED TO LEARN SO MUCH MORE ABOUT YOU.

PRECIOUS HOLY SPIRIT I NEED TO TASTE YOU. PLEASE LET MY SPIRIT THIRST AND CRAVE MORE AND MORE FOR YOU.

PRECIOUS HOLY SPIRIT I NEED TO EMBRACE YOU. I NEED YOUR AMAZING GRACE TO ENDURE THIS ETERNAL RACE WITH YOU.

PRECIOUS HOLY SPIRIT I NEED TO KNOW YOU. PLEASE TEACH ME EVERYTHING THERE IS TO KNOW ABOUT YOU.

PRECIOUS HOLY SPIRIT PLEASE COME INTO MY LIFE AND HAVE YOUR WAY EACH AND EVERY DAY. SPIRIT OF THE LIVING GOD, I LONG TO DO MY FATHER'S WILL. SPIRIT OF THE LIVING GOD, I LONG TO DO MY SAVIOURS WILL. SPIRIT OF THE LIVING GOD, I LONG TO DO THY PERFECT WILL. PRECIOUS HOLY SPIRIT, PLEASE TEACH ME EACH AND EVERY DAY, I PRAY TO WALK IN YOUR PERFECT WAY. I ASK THIS IN THE MIGHTY NAME OF JESUS. AMEN AND AMEN.

I WILL SEEK YOU PRECIOUS HOLY SPIRIT

EVERY SECOND I TAKE A BREATH, HELP ME TO SEEK YOU WITH ALL OF MY HEART PRECIOUS HOLY SPIRIT.

EVERY HOUR OF THE DAY, HELP ME TO BREATHE YOU AND TO SEEK YOU PRECIOUS HOLY SPIRIT.

EVERY DAY OF THE WEEK, HELP ME TO SEEK YOU AND TO BECOME MORE LIKE YOU PRECIOUS HOLY SPIRIT.

EVERY WEEK OF THE MONTH, HELP ME TO SEEK YOU AND TO KNOW YOU BETTER PRECIOUS HOLY SPIRIT.

EVERY MONTH OF THE YEAR, HELP ME TO SEEK YOU AND TO LIVE WITHOUT FEAR PRECIOUS HOLY SPIRIT.

EVERY YEAR, HELP ME TO SEEK YOU PRECIOUS HOLY SPIRIT, AS YOU SHOW ME HOW MUCH YOU CARE PRECIOUS HOLY SPIRIT.

THROUGHOUT THE ENDLESS AGES, I WILL SEEK YOU PRECIOUS HOLY SPIRIT BECAUSE YOU GIVE LIFE PRECIOUS HOLY SPIRIT.

EVERY HOUR OF EVERY DAY, EVERY DAY OF EVERY WEEK, EVERY WEEK OF EVERY MONTH AND EVERY MONTH OF EVERY YEAR I WILL SEEK YOU PRECIOUS HOLY SPIRIT, AND THROUGHOUT THE ENDLESS AGES, I WILL SEEK YOUR FACE PRECIOUS HOLY SPIRIT BECAUSE YOU GIVE LIFE. AMEN AND AMEN.

PRECIOUS HOLY SPIRIT I AM CONSULTING YOU

PRECIOUS HOLY SPIRIT I AM CONSULTING YOU, PLEASE SHOW ME WHAT TO DO. PRECIOUS HOLY SPIRIT I AM CONSULTING YOU, PLEASE SHOW ME THE THINGS THAT ARE FROM YOU.

PRECIOUS HOLY SPIRIT I AM CONSULTING YOU, PLEASE SHOW ME THE STRAIGHT AND NARROW WAY. PRECIOUS HOLY SPIRIT I AM CONSULTING YOU, PLEASE SHOW ME THE ETERNAL PRICE THAT MY PRECIOUS JESUS DID PAY.

PRECIOUS HOLY SPIRIT I AM CONSULTING YOU, PLEASE SHOW ME THE THINGS OF MY PRECIOUS HOLY FATHER. PRECIOUS HOLY SPIRIT I AM CONSULTING YOU, PLEASE SHOW ME THE HEART OF MY PRECIOUS HOLY FATHER.

PRECIOUS HOLY SPIRIT I AM CONSULTING YOU, PLEASE SHOW ME YOUR ETERNAL PLAN. PRECIOUS HOLY SPIRIT I AM CONSULTING YOU, PLEASE SHOW ME AND HELP ME TO UNDERSTAND.

PRECIOUS HOLY SPIRIT I AM CONSULTING YOU, PLEASE SHOW ME THE MIND OF CHRIST. PRECIOUS HOLY SPIRIT I AM CONSULTING YOU, PLESAE SHOW ME HIS ETERNAL SACRIFICE.

PRECIOUS HOLY SPIRIT I AM CONSULTING YOU, PLEASE SHOW ME THE WORDS I SHOULD SAY. PRECIOUS HOLY SPIRIT I AM CONSULTING YOU, PLEASE SHOW ME YOUR WORDS EACH AND EVERY DAY.

PRECIOUS HOLY SPIRIT I AM CONSULTING YOU, PLEASE SHOWER ME WITH YOUR ETERNAL LOVE. PRECIOUS HOLY SPIRIT I AM CONSULTING YOU, PLEASE SHOW ME AND REST ON ME JUST LIKE A GENTLE DOVE.

PRECIOUS HOLY SPIRIT I AM CONSULTING YOU, WHAT ELSE CAN I DO. PRECIOUS HOLY SPIRIT I AM CONSULTING YOU BECAUSE I AM OH SO DESPERATE ONLY FOR YOU. PRECIOUS HOLY SPIRIT I INVITE YOU INTO MY LIFE, PRECIOUS HOLY SPIRIT PLEASE STAY WITHIN MY SIGHT. I THANK YOU PRECIOUS HOLY SPIRIT IN THE PRECIOUS NAME OF JESUS. AMEN AND AMEN.

PLEASE FILL ME PRECIOUS HOLY SPIRIT UNTIL I OVER FLOW

PLEASE FILL ME PRECIOUS HOLY SPIRIT UNTIL I OVER FLOW,
PLEASE FILL ME AND TEACH ME HOW TO GROW.

PLEASE FILL ME PRECIOUS HOLY SPIRIT UNTIL I OVER FLOW,
PLEASE LEAD ME TO THE PATH WHERE I MUST GO.

PLEASE FILL ME PRECIOUS HOLY SPIRIT UNTIL I OVER FLOW,
PLEASE GUIDE AND HELP ME TO FLOW.

PLEASE FILL ME PRECIOUS HOLY SPIRIT UNTIL I OVER FLOW,
PLEASE ALLOW YOUR LOVE IN ME TO SHOW.

PLEASE FILL ME PRECIOUS HOLY SPIRIT UNTIL I OVER FLOW,
PLEASE REFRESH ME SO I CAN GLOW.

PLEASE FILL ME PRECIOUS HOLY SPIRIT UNTIL I OVER FLOW,
PLEASE RELEASE ME ON THY RIVERS TO ROW.

PLEASE FILL ME PRECIOUS HOLY SPIRIT UNTIL I OVER FLOW,
PLEASE FILL ME WITH YOUR STATUS QUO.

PRECIOUS HOLY SPIRIT, I AM DESPERATE TO BE FILLED BY YOU,
I AM DESPERATE TO BE GUIDED BY YOU AND I AM DESPERATE
TO BE FED BY YOU. SPIRIT OF THE LIVING GOD, PLEASE
LEAD ME INTO ALL YOUR TRUTHS. I ASK THIS IN THE MOST
PRECIOUS NAME OF JESUS. AMEN AND AMEN.

I BREATHE YOU PRECIOUS HOLY SPIRIT

I BREATHE IN THE LIFE THAT YOU GIVE TO ME SPIRIT OF THE LIVING GOD. THEREFORE, I BREATHE YOU.

I BREATHE IN THE LOVE THAT YOU GIVE TO ME SPIRIT OF THE LIVING GOD. THEREFORE, I BREATHE YOU.

I BREATHE IN THE HEALTH THAT YOU GIVE TO ME SPIRIT OF THE LIVING GOD. THEREFORE, I BREATHE YOU.

I BREATHE IN THE WISDOM THAT YOU GIVE TO ME SPIRIT OF THE LIVING GOD. THEREFORE, I BREATHE YOU.

I BREATHE IN THE WEALTH THAT YOU GIVE TO ME SPIRIT OF THE LIVING GOD. THEREFORE, I BREATHE YOU.

I BREATHE IN THE HOPE THAT YOU GIVE TO ME SPIRIT OF THE LIVING GOD. THEREFORE, I BREATHE YOU.

I BREATHE IN THE ETERNAL HOPE THAT YOU GIVE TO ME SPIRIT OF THE LIVING GOD. THEREFORE, I BREATHE YOU.

WITH EVERY BREATH THAT I TAKE, I BREATHE YOU PRECIOUS HOLY FATHER, I BREATHE YOU PRECIOUS LORD JESUS AND I BREATHE YOU PRECIOUS HOLY SPIRIT. I THANK YOU FOR SHOWING ME THE FULNESS OF LIFE I HAVE IN YOU, SPIRIT OF THE LIVING GOD. AMEN AND AMEN.

PLEASE SHOW ME WHERE MY BLESSINGS ARE PRECIOUS HOLY SPIRIT

PLEASE SHOW ME WHERE MY BLESSINGS ARE PRECIOUS HOLY SPIRIT, I NEED TO KNOW. PLEASE SHOW ME WHERE MY BLESSINGS ARE PRECIOUS HOLY SPIRIT BECAUSE I NEED TO GROW.

PLEASE SHOW ME WHERE MY BLESSINGS ARE PRECIOUS HOLY SPIRIT, I NEED TO SEE. PLEASE SHOW ME WHERE MY BLESSINGS ARE PRECIOUS HOLY SPIRIT BECAUSE I NEED TO SEE WHERE I CAN BE SET FREE.

PLEASE SHOW ME WHERE MY BLESSINGS ARE PRECIOUS HOLY SPIRIT, I NEED TO TASTE. PLEASE SHOW ME WHERE MY BLESSINGS ARE PRECIOUS HOLY SPIRIT BECAUSE I NEED TO NEGATE ALL THIS WASTE.

PLEASE SHOW ME WHERE MY BLESSINGS ARE PRECIOUS HOLY SPIRIT, I NEED TO CARE. PLEASE SHOW ME WHERE MY BLESSINGS ARE PRECIOUS HOLY SPIRIT BECAUSE I NEED IT SO I CAN SHARE.

PLEASE SHOW ME WHERE MY BLESSINGS ARE PRECIOUS HOLY SPIRIT, I NEED TO FIND IT. PLEASE SHOW ME WHERE MY BLESSINGS ARE PRECIOUS HOLY SPIRIT BECAUSE YOU HAVE ALREADY SIGNED IT.

PLEASE SHOW ME WHERE MY BLESSINGS ARE PRECIOUS HOLY SPIRIT, I NEED TO REJOICE. PLEASE SHOW ME WHERE MY BLESSINGS ARE PRECIOUS HOLY SPIRIT BECAUSE YOU ARE MY PERFECT CHOICE.

PLEASE SHOW ME WHERE MY BLESSINGS ARE PRECIOUS HOLY SPIRIT, I NEED TO KNOW. PLEASE SHOW ME WHERE MY BLESSINGS ARE PRECIOUS HOLY SPIRIT BECAUSE I NEED TO MAKE YOUR BLESSINGS FLOW.

1 CORINTHIANS 2:9 NIV "However, as it is written: "What no eye has seen, what no ear has heard, and what no human mind has conceived"— the things God has prepared for those who love him."

PRECIOUS HOLY SPIRIT I ASK YOU TO TAKE ME TO THAT PLACE AND ALLOW ME TO LIVE BY MY FATHER'S GRACE. I ASK THIS IN THE MOST PRECIOUS NAME OF JESUS. AMEN AND AMEN.